NAIMA ABDULLAH

ETERNAL MESSAGES FROM THE QURAN

Edited by:

Amel S. Abdullah

Cover by:

Naafi Nur Rohma

بسم الله الرحمن الرحيم

IN THE NAME OF ALLAH

Introduction

Whenever my family and I are having a meal together, my respected father (may Allāh ﷻ bless and reward him greatly) frequently brings up a verse from the Qur'ān as a topic for discussion for all of us to reflect upon and think about on a deeper level. This good habit, ingrained in me since childhood, is one of the main things that has inspired me to learn more about Allāh's Holy Book, The Glorious Qur'ān.

There are many hidden gems and treasures in the Qur'ān that one should strive to discover so long as one is alive—and sharing what you have learned with others holds great rewards. When we start with our families, we create a domino effect that spreads throughout our communities as more people gain knowledge of the Qur'ān and come to understand how its eternal lessons can be applied to our lives on a practical level.

That's why I was overjoyed to learn that some of my beloved readers have been sharing the passages in my first book ("Islam Taught Me") with their children and other family members. Please continue doing this as you read the current volume, which is focused solely on the Qur'ān. The passages are deliberately short, containing simple yet profound messages that readers of all ages and backgrounds can (by Allāh's will) appreciate and relate to.

Among other things, the book's passages contain inspirational thoughts, heartfelt stories from the Qur'ān to reflect upon, and even a couple of fun exercises to apply in relation to the quoted material.

It should be mentioned that many of the 120 short verses from the Qur'ān you are about to read were selected with the kind assistance of the respected publisher of this book (Br. Mouad Garwan), who has been a pleasure to work with on this and other beneficial projects. In addition, I greatly benefited from the help and advice of my mother as she edited the English-language edition of the book.

According to my mother, who is herself a convert to Islām, there are certain turning points in all of our lives when we must make conscious decisions regarding the path we wish to follow, and consistently making the right decisions will eventually lead one to Islām and true belief in Allāh ﷻ. Each time we deviate, however, we needlessly delay our journey on the path of righteousness as we struggle to find our way back. My father has also taught me that positive change begins in one's own self with the deliberate small decisions we make each and every day during our short time on Earth—but we need to act quickly, as tomorrow is not guaranteed for any of us.

With these thoughts in mind, allow me to draw attention to a very important Qur'ānic verse that I hope you will remember as you read through all of this book's passages:

وَٱلَّذِينَ جَٰهَدُواْ فِينَا لَنَهۡدِيَنَّهُمۡ سُبُلَنَاۚ وَإِنَّ ٱللَّهَ لَمَعَ ٱلۡمُحۡسِنِينَ

"And those who strive for Us - We will surely guide them to Our ways.[1] And indeed, Allāh is with the doers of good."

— *Sūrat al-'Ankabūt (Qur'ān 29:69)*

1. The path of true guidance that allows one to attain Allāh's pleasure in this life, leading to success in the Hereafter.

I have personally felt the truth of this verse throughout the different stages of my life. Positive Islamic changes to one's character, personality, and lifestyle may seem difficult, or even impossible, when a person's good intentions remain confined to the realm of the theoretical, but when one takes concrete steps to actually implement the desired changes, Allāh ﷻ opens many doors of blessings and ease along the road.

Before I leave you to take your personal journey inside of this book, I would like to share another thought with you that I hope will motivate you to enhance your relationship with the Qur'ān.

Life sometimes takes us to strange places, and we frequently have to deal with complicated situations, personalities, challenges, and doubts—but the Qur'ān resolves it all; if you are already a believer, it will deepen your belief, while if you harbor doubts of any kind, it will give you certainty and tranquility, because it speaks directly to your mind.

If you enjoy and benefit from this book (which I pray you do, *in shā' Allāh*), remember that this only **a small glimpse into the eternal messages of the Great Qur'ān!**

Finally, may Allāh ﷻ accept this work and reward everyone who made it possible for this book to be published (and Allāh ﷻ is The Grantor of All Success).

— Naima Abdullah

وَكَذَٰلِكَ نُنْجِي الْمُؤْمِنِينَ

Wa-ka-dhālika nunjī l-muʾminīn

"And thus do We save the believers."

— Sūrat al-Anbiyāʾ (Qurʾān 21:88)

Don't worry.

Your financial issues will be solved.

The illness that you or your loved ones have been suffering from is going to be alleviated.

Harassment, oppression, psychological pressure, family problems, work problems...

Personal problems...

They shall all fade away if you are a believer in Allāh!

Turn to Allāh ﷻ, and He will save you...

Just like He saved Prophet Yūnus (Jonah) (PBUH) from the fish that swallowed him...

And just like He saved Prophet Mūsá (Moses) (PBUH) and the believers from the oppressive pharaoh of their time (Firʿawn).

قَدْ أَفْلَحَ الْمُؤْمِنُونَ

Qad ʾaflaḥa l-muʾminūn

"Certainly will the believers have succeeded."

— *Sūrat al-Muʾminūn (Qurʾān 23:1)*

For some people, success is measured by the number of likes or compliments they receive on an Instagram post, or by the trendy clothes they are able to buy. For others, success might mean marriage to someone beautiful or wealthy, a dream job, or another worldly achievement.

But let this verse be a reminder to them—and to you and me alike—about the true definition of success:

Striving to remain spiritually healthy at a time when immorality and materialism is both desired and widespread.

You have succeeded each time you:

- Commit to your prayers and submit to Allāh ﷻ despite any worldly distractions;
- Refrain from idle talk, *ḥarām* relationships, and immodest wear despite all of the temptations;
- Stay honest despite the corruption all around us.

Those who adopt the above qualities are the "inheritors" Allāh ﷻ promises "will inherit al-Firdaws [the highest part of Paradise]," where "they will abide therein eternally."[2]

2. Qur'ān 23:10–11.

لَا تَتَّبِعُوا خُطُوَاتِ الشَّيْطَانِ

Lā tattabiʿū khuṭuwāti sh-shayṭān

"Do not follow the footsteps of Satan."

— *Sūrat al-Nūr (Qurʾān 24:21)*

How your life goes is all about the steps you take.

If you wish to cultivate a healthy lifestyle, for example, you will gradually stop all of your bad habits and replace them with good ones until your good habits become a way of life.

At first, you might only exercise once a week, then twice a week, and then every other day before you finally make it to the gym every day.

If you wish to protect your heart from corruption:

Don't stop your daily reading of the Qurʾān...

Don't stop waking up early to pray Fajr...

Don't abandon the positive habits you already have, such as smiling to people, checking up on them, and visiting them or helping them as much as you can.

Protect your tongue from gossip.

Protect your eyes and ears from watching or listening to the things that are *ḥarām*, and remember:

Small steps often lead to bigger steps that create habitual changes that change the soul.

إِنَّهُ هُوَ الْغَفُورُ الرَّحِيمُ

ʾInnahū huwa l-ghafūru r-raḥīmm

"Indeed, it is He who is the Forgiving, the Merciful."

— *Sūrat al-Zumar (Qurʾān 39:53)*

We feel happy when our loved ones forgive us for a mistake we made.

But Allāh ﷻ does not only forgive us for our mistakes...

He is "**The** Forgiving!"

So, why is there so much despair in your heart?

Do you think (Allāh forbid) that your sins can't be forgiven?

Don't you feel happy when you learn that your Muslim sister started to wear the *ḥijāb*? Or that someone started praying or stopped a *ḥarām* act for the sake of Allāh ﷻ?

Allāh ﷻ is even more delighted with your repentance!

So, cheer up, and go make *wuḍūʾ*; it's an important first step that helps start the process of washing away one's sins.

فَمَنِ اهْتَدَىٰ فَلِنَفْسِهِ وَمَن ضَلَّ فَإِنَّمَا يَضِلُّ عَلَيْهَا

Fa-mani htadā fa-li-nafsihī wa-man ḍalla
fa-ʾinnamā yaḍillu ʿalayhā

"So whoever is guided - it is for [the benefit of] his soul; and whoever goes astray only goes astray to its detriment."

— *Sūrat al-Zumar (Qurʾān 39:41)*

Praying five times a day is a continuous reminder that purifies you from engaging in acts that destroy the soul.

Being fair, just, truthful, respectful, and kind to others gives you peace of mind and improves the quality of your sleep, in addition to making you gain the love of Allāh ﷻ and people.

Wearing the *ḥijāb* protects you from unpleasant interactions and improves your relationship with Allāh ﷻ.

Fasting and reading the Qurʾān shield your heart from spiritual illnesses like arrogance and selfishness.

The path you take is your choice, and only you will bear its consequences.

So, which path are you going to choose?

وَلَوْ أَنَّ لِلَّذِينَ ظَلَمُوا۟ مَا فِي ٱلْأَرْضِ جَمِيعًا وَمِثْلَهُۥ مَعَهُۥ لَٱفْتَدَوْا۟
بِهِۦ مِن سُوٓءِ ٱلْعَذَابِ يَوْمَ ٱلْقِيَٰمَةِ

Wa-law ʾanna li-lladhīna ẓalamū mā fī l-ʾarḍi jamīʿan wa-mithlahū maʿahū la-ftadaw bihī min sūʾi l-ʿadhābi yawma l-qiyāmah

"And if those who did wrong had all that is in the earth entirely and the like of it with it, they would [attempt to] ransom themselves thereby from the worst of the punishment on the Day of Resurrection."

— *Sūrat al-Zumar (Qurʾān 39:47)*

Because Allāh ﷻ is The Utterly Just and The Giver of Justice, He will not overlook the harm that comes from causing harm to others (through cheating, lying, bullying, blackmailing, and other sinful behaviors).

Before you transgress against another person, ask yourself how you want to stand in front of your Lord ﷻ **on the Day when it is only your deeds and intentions that matter.**

لَا يَعۡزُبُ عَنۡهُ مِثۡقَالُ ذَرَّةٖ فِي ٱلسَّمَٰوَٰتِ وَلَا فِي ٱلۡأَرۡضِ
وَلَآ أَصۡغَرُ مِن ذَٰلِكَ وَلَآ أَكۡبَرُ

Lā yaʿzubu ʿanhu mithqālu dharratin
fī s-samāwāti wa-lā fī l-ʾarḍi wa-lā ʾaṣgharu
min dhālika wa-lā ʾakbar

"Not absent from Him is an atom's weight within the heavens or within the earth or [what is] smaller than that or greater."

— *Sūrat Saba' (Qur'ān 34:3)*

If you were sure that a trustworthy authority in your workplace knew about everything going on there and was able to distinguish between the hard-working employees and the office "troublemakers," wouldn't you feel privileged, safe, and comfortable regardless of any problems your co-workers tried to cause for you?

If so, don't forget the fact that each and every one of us has a much greater privilege with the Creator!

All of the good intentions hidden inside of our hearts, the efforts we thought that nobody noticed, and the people we secretly made smile...

Our patience despite the harsh words from someone we loved or respected and the unfair treatment we received...

Our attempts at improving our faith, and how we don't give up even though it is sometimes very difficult...

Every single one of these things is known to The Knower of the unseen!

This is how Allāh ﷻ rewards "those who believe and do righteous deeds" providing them with "forgiveness and noble provision,"[3] while the wrongdoers who may have thought that their evil acts were concealed will have no shelter from Allāh ﷻ.

3. Qur'ān 34:4.

اَعْمَلُوٓا۟ ءَالَ دَاوُۥدَ شُكْرًا

I'malū āla dāwūda shukra

"Work, O family of Dā'ūd, in gratitude."

— *Sūrat Saba' (Qur'ān 34:13)*

When someone does you a favor, brings you a gift, or is basically a good friend to you, it is only natural for you to also be generous with that person and express your gratitude in a way that goes beyond mere words.

If we have such feelings toward the everyday, "ordinary" people in our lives, how should we go about thanking Allāh ﷻ (Who is even much more worthy of our gratitude) for all of the blessings He has given us?

The best answer to this question lies in the verse quoted above.

Make use of the blessings you have by obeying Allāh ﷻ.

If Allāh ﷻ has gifted you with the talent of writing, let your pen flow in a way that pleases Him, whether you write a novel, an essay, or a short story.

If you have parents, be kind to them, and help them as much as you can.

Do not let money corrupt your way of life.

Do as the verse says, and work in gratitude.

فَقَالُواْ رَبَّنَا بَٰعِدۡ بَيۡنَ أَسۡفَارِنَا وَظَلَمُوٓاْ أَنفُسَهُمۡ فَجَعَلۡنَٰهُمۡ أَحَادِيثَ

Fa-qālū rabbanā bāʿid bayna ʾasfārinā wa-ẓalamū ʾanfusahum fa-jaʿalnāhum ʾaḥādīth

"But [insolently] they said, 'Our Lord, lengthen the distance between our journeys,' and wronged themselves, so We made them narrations [cautionary tales as lessons to others]."

— *Sūrat Sabaʾ (Qurʾān 34:19)*

Don't be like the people of Sabaʾ (Sheba),[4] who ended up losing everything when they ungratefully threw away all of the privileges and blessings Allāh ﷻ had given them.

Thank Allāh ﷻ for the home you have, and for the people around you.

Instead of complaining all the time about your studies or work, thank Allāh ﷻ for all that you have been able to accomplish in life.

Thank Allāh ﷻ for the ability to walk, think, and speak.

Whenever you find yourself complaining about something, remember the countless blessings in that very same thing you are complaining about!

---

4. As described in the Qurʾān, the people of Sabaʾ (in Yemen) were living a blessed life with gardens all around them—and even their travel-routes were dotted with nearby cities that made travel safe and easy for them. But they were ungrateful for these blessings and insolently asked Allāh ﷻ to make the distances between the cities further away, as shown in the above verse.

Always teach yourself to have satisfaction, and you will never go wrong.

وَمَآ أَنفَقْتُم مِّن شَيْءٍ فَهُوَ يُخْلِفُهُۥ

Wa-mā 'anfaqtum min shay'in fa-huwa yukhlifuh

"But whatever thing you spend [in His cause] - He will compensate it."

— *Sūrat Saba' (Qur'ān 34:39)*

Don't hesitate to give.

Whatever you give will not go to waste.

Think of it as a noble exchange between you and Allāh ﷻ, The Best of Providers.

Not only will He compensate you and bless your money, but He will also wash away your sins and answer your supplications.

And remember that charity is not only limited to money; **it could also be a kind word that soothes someone's pain.**

إِنِّي أَخَافُ أَن يُبَدِّلَ دِينَكُمْ أَوْ أَن يُظْهِرَ فِي الْأَرْضِ الْفَسَادَ

ʾInnī ʾakhāfu ʾan yubaddila dīnakum ʾaw ʾan yuẓhira fī l-ʾarḍi l-fasād

"Indeed, I fear that he will change your religion or that he will cause corruption in the land."

— Sūrat Ghāfir (Qurʾān 40:26)

You may be surprised when you learn that this statement was actually made by Firʿawn to his people in reference to Prophet Mūsá (Moses) (PBUH).

But this is actually how some people are!

Someone may hurt you deeply and then go around warning others, claiming that you are the one who is causing trouble!

Don't expect that everyone will automatically like and praise you when you live your life in a way that is pleasing to Allāh ﷻ.

You may be bullied, avoided, or lied about for this very reason!

This is when you have to be strong, just like our prophets (peace be upon them all) were as they dealt with their corrupted nations.

يُرِيدُونَ لِيُطْفِـُٔوا۟ نُورَ ٱللَّهِ بِأَفْوَٰهِهِمْ وَٱللَّهُ مُتِمُّ نُورِهِۦ

Yurīdūna li-yuṭfiʾū nūra llāhi bi-ʾafwāhihim
wa-llāhu mutimmu nūrih

"They want to extinguish the light of Allāh with their mouths, but Allāh will perfect His light."

— *Sūrat al-Ṣaff (Qurʾān 61:8)*

This is basically because the religion of Allāh ﷻ perfectly aligns with a person's *fiṭrah* (natural inclination toward the truth).

People may sometimes lie, but the truth will always eventually prevail, because it is against human nature to lie.

It may sometimes feel like everyone is going astray these days, especially in this age of unfiltered news and social media.

You may feel like it is pointless to stick to your Islamic principles when nearly everything immoral has become so normalized in this increasingly chaotic world of ours.

This is when you should remember that the challenges faced by the prophets and other righteous believers who lived before us were not any easier.

Since the beginning of humanity, it has always been a battle between good and evil in different forms.

What is certain, however, is that Allāh's light is what always prevails in the end, as Allāh ﷻ shows us in the Qurʾān's many stories.

وَمِنَ اللَّيْلِ فَسَبِّحْهُ

Wa-mina l-layli fa-sabbiḥh

"And [in part] of the night exalt Him."

— *Sūrat Qāf (Qur'ān 50:40)*

For many people, the period before one falls asleep at night can be very distressing, because it is a time when negative thoughts that have been suppressed throughout the day commonly begin to emerge.

Don't drown in these thoughts.

Several verses in the Qur'ān emphasize the remembrance of Allāh ﷻ at night.

This remembrance is the best remedy for negative thoughts, providing a much-needed distraction from the darkness of the night.

فَاصْبِرْ كَمَا صَبَرَ أُولُو الْعَزْمِ مِنَ الرُّسُلِ

Fa-ṣbir ka-mā ṣabara ʾulū l-ʿazmi mina r-rusul

"So be patient, as were those of determination among the messengers."

— *Sūrat al-Aḥqāf (Qurʾān 46:35)*

Things take time.

If you are just starting to learn a particular skill, don't expect to be a pro right from the start.

Leave some space for trial and error...

To learn...

To grow.

If the prophets had given up with the first difficulties they faced, the religion of Islām would not have reached us today!

The most important thing is to continue.

إِن تَنصُرُوا اللَّهَ يَنصُرْكُمْ

'In tanṣurū llāha yanṣurkum

"If you support Allāh, He will support you."

— *Sūrat Muḥammad (Qur'ān 47:7)*

Do you wish to have the support of Allāh ﷻ in your daily affairs?

The way to achieve that is apparent in the above verse.

Be a truthful and sincere representative of Islām...

And you shall not have anything to fear.

وَٱلَّذِينَ ءَامَنُواْ وَعَمِلُواْ ٱلصَّٰلِحَٰتِ وَءَامَنُواْ بِمَا نُزِّلَ عَلَىٰ مُحَمَّدٍ وَهُوَ
ٱلْحَقُّ مِن رَّبِّهِمْ كَفَّرَ عَنْهُمْ سَيِّـَٔاتِهِمْ وَأَصْلَحَ بَالَهُمْ

Wa-lladhīna ʾāmanū wa-ʿamilū ṣ-ṣāliḥāti wa-ʾāmanū bi-mā nuzzila ʿalā muḥammadin wa-huwa l-ḥaqqu min rabbihim kaffara ʿanhum sayyiʾātihim wa-ʾaṣlaḥa bālahum

"And those who believe and do righteous deeds and believe in what has been sent down upon Muḥammad - and it is the truth from their Lord - He will remove from them their misdeeds and amend their condition."

— *Sūrat Muḥammad (Qurʾān 47:2)*

Starting from today, make it a goal to really understand the words that Allāh ﷻ revealed to Prophet Muḥammad ﷺ in the Qurʾān.

Read a page each day.

Learn the vocabulary and story associated with each verse.

Write down something you have learned from the verses you've read, and make note of what you would like to start practicing.

Finally, make a check-list to keep track of all the new habits you wish to introduce to your life.

This is a fun approach that helps motivate one into living the values of Islām and the Qur'ān rather than only reading about them.

Try it, and then tell your friends about it, too!

May Allāh ﷻ bless and guide us all.

قَالَ أَوَلَوْ جِئْتُكُم بِأَهْدَىٰ مِمَّا وَجَدتُّمْ عَلَيْهِ آبَاءَكُمْ قَالُوا إِنَّا بِمَا أُرْسِلْتُم بِهِ كَافِرُونَ

Qāla ʾa-wa-law jiʾtukum bi-ʾahdā mimmā wajadtum ʿalayhi ʾābāʾakum qālū ʾinnā bi-mā ʾursiltum bihī kāfirūn

"[Each warner] said, 'Even if I brought you better guidance than that [religion] upon which you found your fathers?' They said, 'Indeed we, in that with which you were sent, are disbelievers.'"

— *Sūrat al-Zukhruf (Qurʾān 43:24)*

Although a lot of wisdom and other positive things can be learned from our respected elders, some of their inherited habits and traditions may also be displeasing to Allāh ﷻ.

Whenever you find this to be the case, do what is needed to make changes in your own habits and traditions so that they become compatible with true Islamic values. Faithfully adhering to the teachings of Islām can only be of benefit to both you and future generations of believers who will one day learn from your example.

Otherwise, how different are we from those nations mentioned in the Qurʾān whose people refused guidance under the pretense of blindly following the traditions of their fathers?

When the Qurʾān is your judge, the path will be much easier than you can imagine.

وَلَوْلَآ أَن يَكُونَ ٱلنَّاسُ أُمَّةً وَٰحِدَةً لَّجَعَلْنَا لِمَن يَكْفُرُ بِٱلرَّحْمَٰنِ
لِبُيُوتِهِمْ سُقُفًا مِّن فِضَّةٍ وَمَعَارِجَ عَلَيْهَا يَظْهَرُونَ

Wa-law-lā ʾan yakūna n-nāsu ʾummatan wāḥidatan la-jaʿalnā li-man yakfuru bi-r-raḥmāni li-buyūtihim suqufan min fiḍḍatin wa-maʿārija ʿalayhā yaẓharūn

"And if it were not that the people would become one community, We would have made for those who disbelieve in the Most Merciful - for their houses - ceilings and stairways of silver upon which to mount."

— *Sūrat al-Zukhruf (Qurʾān 43:33)*

This verse is an answer to those who claim that wealth is a sign of Allāh's approval.

Sometimes you may see blatantly corrupt people living a life of extreme comfort and luxury while claiming to be among the righteous.

Don't be overwhelmed by what they have; wealth is actually one of the hardest tests a person can have in this worldly life.

If you had all that money, would you still be humble and always remain committed to your Islamic values?

Would you spend your money on charity and beneficial projects?

Or would you become materialistic and show off your wealth to others?

As Allāh ﷻ tells us in a subsequent verse:

"But all that [luxury] is not but the enjoyment of worldly life. And the Hereafter with your Lord is for the righteous."[5]

5. Qur'ān 43:35.

وَإِنَّهُمْ لَيَصُدُّونَهُمْ عَنِ ٱلسَّبِيلِ وَيَحْسَبُونَ أَنَّهُم مُّهْتَدُونَ

Wa-ʾinnahum la-yaṣuddūnahum ʿani s-sabīli wa-yaḥsabūna ʾannahum muhtadūn

"And indeed, they [i.e., the devils] avert them from the way [of guidance] while they think that they are [rightly] guided."

— *Sūrat al-Zukhruf (Qurʾān 43:37)*

Someone who follows the footsteps of Satan will soon find that Satan has become his or her constant companion, whispering evil thoughts as he justifies the unjustified and makes what is prohibited to us seem attractive.

In order to protect yourself from falling into such a trap, here are some things to re-evaluate every once in a while:

- **What your mind is preoccupied with** (Do you spend most of your time on worldly matters, such as what to eat, wear, or buy? Or do you reserve ample time for worship and set worthwhile goals that will benefit you in the Hereafter?)
- **Your prayers** (Do you pray on time? Are you distracted when you pray?)
- **Your morals** (Are you being respectful with others? Are you still humble and caring? Or are you interrupting, cyber-bullying, and blocking everyone? What about your day-to-day activities? Do you avoid being in the places that displease Allāh ﷻ?)

If you notice that your behaviors do not align with your actual beliefs and values and what you know to be right, **then you should carefully inspect the footsteps you have been following lately, before it is too late!**

فَجَآءَتْهُ إِحْدَىٰهُمَا تَمْشِي عَلَى ٱسْتِحْيَآءٍ

Fa-jā'athu 'iḥdāhumā tamshī 'alā stiḥyā'

"Then one of the two women came to him [Mūsá] walking with shyness."

— *Sūrat al-Qaṣaṣ (Qur'ān 28:25)*

Shyness is the adornment of men and women alike.

You become more attractive each time you:

- Use respectable speech;
- Speak in a moderate and humble tone;
- Set boundaries when dealing with the opposite gender;
- Take care not to embarrass someone, even when the opportunity is present;
- Dress modestly;
- Refuse to engage in *ḥarām*.

Remember the words of Prophet Muḥammad ﷺ, who said that "*al-ḥayā'* (shyness) is a branch of faith."[6]

6. *Ṣaḥīḥ Muslim*, No. 35a.

وَقَالُوا لَوْلَا نُزِّلَ هَٰذَا الْقُرْآنُ عَلَىٰ رَجُلٍ مِّنَ الْقَرْيَتَيْنِ عَظِيمٍ

Wa-qālū law-lā nuzzila hādhā l-qur'ānu
'alā rajulin mina l-qaryatayni 'aẓīm

"And they said, 'Why was this Qur'ān not sent down upon a great man from [one of] the two cities?'"

— *Sūrat al-Zukhruf (Qur'ān 43:31)*

You may be unfairly rejected at job interviews.

People may even try their best to discourage you when they see that you are succeeding.

Don't be sad when people try to diminish your worth.

The pagans of Makkah tried such tactics with the best of all men on Earth, Muḥammad ﷺ!

The people who did this knew deep inside that the Prophet ﷺ had come with the truth from Allāh ﷻ, and they actually loved and respected him for his good values—but it was their arrogance that made them take this approach.

Did the Prophet ﷺ stop? Did he give up?

No, he did not, for one simple reason: **he knew that Allāh ﷻ was with him.**

سَنَشُدُّ عَضُدَكَ بِأَخِيكَ

Sa-nashuddu ʿaḍudaka bi-ʾakhīk

"We will strengthen your arm through your brother."

— *Sūrat al-Qaṣaṣ (Qur'ān 28:35)*

The best friendships are those that make you stronger...

Stronger in faith and in your ability to face the world.

Such friendships remind you to be patient and see the good in situations, like when Prophet Muḥammad ﷺ comforted his best friend and Companion, Abū Bakr al-Ṣiddīq (RA), by saying: "Do not grieve; indeed Allāh is with us."[7]

A friend might also be your brother, like Hārūn (Aaron) was to Mūsá (Moses) (peace be upon them both), the brothers mentioned in the above verse.

Friendship can also be found in marriage, like the example of Khadījah (RA) comforting the Prophet ﷺ when he came to her shaking after his first interaction with the heavens.

If you and your friends are always discouraging each other and spreading negativity, it may be time to re-evaluate **the sincerity of these friendships.**

7. Qur'ān 9:40.

ٱلْأَخِلَّآءُ يَوْمَئِذٍۭ بَعْضُهُمْ لِبَعْضٍ عَدُوٌّ إِلَّا ٱلْمُتَّقِينَ

L-ʾakhillāʾu yawmaʾidhin baʿḍuhum li-baʿḍin ʿaduwwun ʾillā l-muttaqīn

"Close friends, that Day, will be enemies to each other, except for the righteous."

— *Sūrat al-Zukhruf (Qurʾān 43:67)*

My dear, beloved friend:

May Allāh ﷻ bless you for all of the times you said nice words to me, diverted me from my worries, and reminded me that Allāh ﷻ is watching over me.

Thank you for all of the times you reminded me to make *istighfār*[8] and *dhikr*[9] part of my regular worship.

Thank you for encouraging me to pray and read the Qurʾān, as they are the best healers from life's problems.

I was glowing with happiness each time you told me, "I remembered you in my prayers today."

And I remain grateful for all the times you advised me purely for the sake of Allāh ﷻ.

I pray that you and I will be among the righteous "kinds" whom Allāh ﷻ promised will be told on the Day of Judgment:

8. Seeking pardon from Allāh.

9. Remembrance of Allāh.

"O My servants, no fear will there be concerning you this Day, nor will you grieve, [you] who believed in Our verses and were Muslims. Enter Paradise, you and your kinds, delighted."[10]

Send these words in a card, letter, or text to the person who came to mind while reading this.

10. Qur'ān 43:68–70.

هُنَّ لِبَاسٌ لَّكُمْ وَأَنتُمْ لِبَاسٌ لَّهُنَّ

Hunna libāsun lakum wa-'antum libāsun lahunn

"They [your wives] are a garment for you, and you are a garment for them."

— *Sūrat al-Baqarah (Qur'ān 2:187)*

Whether you are male or female, or single, engaged, or married, don't forget that the marital relationship is meant to provide comfort and tranquility to both spouses.

Successful couples put effort into accepting each other's differences as they support one another and overlook any shortcomings.

They make it a habit to smile at each other and thank each other for all of the hard work and nice things each person does.

They listen attentively and respectfully to each other's concerns, even if the topic is not one that would normally interest them.

Most importantly, **they always keep their sacred relationship just between the two of them, with Allāh ﷻ as the third.**

وَالَّذِي قَالَ لِوَالِدَيْهِ أُفٍّ لَّكُمَا

Wa-lladhī qāla li-wālidayhi ʾuffin lakumā

"But one who says to his parents, 'Uff[11] to you...'"

— *Sūrat al-Aḥqāf* (Qur'ān 46:17)

This verse portrays how some young people arrogantly reject or mock their parents' advice, thinking of them as old-fashioned or out-of-touch with the world.

To this young person:

If you happen to meet a child who is much younger than you are and notice that they are harming themselves out of ignorance, wouldn't you want to help them? Wouldn't you feel that they are young, innocent, and still have a lot to learn?

Your parents may not be as knowledgeable about technology as you are, but you should remember that they have much more experience than you do, and they have encountered many situations you know nothing about before you were even born. So, when they advise you, it is due to the instinct of love and care Allāh ﷻ has put in them to guide and protect you.

If something does not make sense to you, discuss it with them politely, but beware of displeasing them, as **"the pleasure of the Lord lies in the pleasure of a parent."**[12]

11. An expression of distaste and irritation.

12. *Sunan al-Tirmidhī*, No. 1899.

وَوَصَّيْنَا ٱلْإِنسَٰنَ بِوَٰلِدَيْهِ إِحْسَٰنًا

Wa-waṣṣaynā l-ʾinsāna bi-wālidayhi ʾiḥsān

"And We have enjoined upon man, to his parents, good treatment."

— *Sūrat al-Aḥqāf (Qur'ān 46:15)*

Your parents are your key to Paradise.

It does not matter what their cultural background, social status, or religion is.

They are the people whom Allāh ﷻ has entrusted us with, just as He entrusted them with us when we were children.

No matter how busy or caught up you are in your life, **don't forget your parents.**

Check on them, sit and chat with them, and supplicate for them.

There is nothing that makes a parent happier than a son or daughter who tries to please them.

وَيَدْرَءُونَ بِٱلْحَسَنَةِ ٱلسَّيِّئَةَ

Wa-yadraʾūna bi-l-ḥasanati s-sayyiʾah

"And they repel evil with good."

— *Sūrat al-Raʿd (Qurʾān 13:22)*

If you have transgressed against another person or even your own self, **don't cry over spilled milk.**

The Qurʾān has given you a practical solution, so replace whatever wrong you committed with a good deed.

Be kind to the people you used to bully or look down at.

Talk about the good qualities of the person you used to backbite.

Give extra charity, and fast extra days with the intention of reforming yourself for the better.

أَلَا بِذِكْرِ ٱللَّهِ تَطْمَئِنُّ ٱلْقُلُوبُ

ʾA-lā bi-dhikri llāhi taṭmaʾinnu l-qulūb

"Unquestionably, by the remembrance of Allāh hearts are assured."

— *Sūrat al-Raʿd (Qurʾān 13:28)*

Because the remembrance of Allāh ﷻ comforts the heart, Allāh ﷻ has made it easy to remember Him throughout the day, making it obligatory for us to pray the five prayers at prescribed times, and teaching us to supplicate and make *dhikr* in almost every situation we encounter.

If you are lazy or reluctant about preforming these rituals, you are missing out on a lot of good things that are important for your own well-being...

And no one is more aware of that than Allāh ﷻ, the One Who created us!

Thank you, Allāh.

أَلَمْ نَجْعَلِ الْأَرْضَ مِهَادًا

ʾA-lam najʿali l-ʾarḍa mihāda

"Have We not made the earth a resting place?"

— Sūrat al-Naba' (Qur'ān 78:6)

O Allāh, Lord of the Worlds...

Thank you for all of the signs you have placed for us on this earth, so that we may discover Your existence, along with Your endless mercy upon us.

Thank you, Allāh...

For making the earth a place where we can walk, build, and harvest our crops...

For giving structure to our days with the blessing of the sun...

And for allowing us to rest and regenerate our energy at night.

I am grateful for all of the different types of plants You allowed the earth to produce for us, and for providing the right environments for them to grow again and again.

There can be no doubt that everything in this vast universe is precisely determined.

أَرَءَيْتَ مَنِ ٱتَّخَذَ إِلَٰهَهُۥ هَوَىٰهُ أَفَأَنتَ تَكُونُ عَلَيْهِ وَكِيلًا

ʾA-raʾayta mani ttakhadha ʾilāhahū hawāhu ʾa-fa-ʾanta takūnu ʿalayhi wakīla

"Have you seen the one who takes as his god his own desire? Then would you be responsible for him?"

— *Sūrat al-Furqān (Qurʾān 25:43)*

One should be aware of the fact that there are people in this world who have made a conscious decision to follow their own desires rather than the path of righteousness that Allāh ﷻ has actually guided us to. In doing so, some have ended up creating new religions for themselves and others in order to serve their evil interests.

"Reminder benefits the believers."[13]

Unfortunately, however, "most people do not believe,"[14] often because they have decided not to see, hear, or use reason, as mentioned in several verses of the Qurʾān.

So, which of the two groups do you wish to belong to?

The majority who, deep inside, recognize Allāh's signs but make a deliberate choice to ignore them, or **the minority who know the truth and also act upon it?**

13. Qurʾān 51:55.

14. Qurʾān 40:59.

اَعْمَلُوا عَلَىٰ مَكَانَتِكُمْ

I'malū 'alā makānatikum

"Work according to your position."

— *Sūrat Hūd (Qur'ān 11:93)*

If you believe that you are worthy of love and respect, then you will seek out the people who accept you for your positive qualities and distance yourself from those who do not recognize your worth.

If you view yourself as a successful person, you will do whatever it takes to achieve your goals.

And if you believe you are a servant of Allāh ﷻ on this earth, then you know what to do...

وَمَا تَوْفِيقِيٓ إِلَّا بِٱللَّهِ

Wa-mā tawfīqī ʾillā bi-llāh

"And my success is not but through Allāh."

— *Sūrat Hūd (Qurʾān 11:88)*

When it comes to the job you have...

And the money you make...

And the academic degree you hold...

And your positive qualities as a human being...

And the knowledge you brag about...

And the love and compliments you receive from others...

And even your strong faith...

They are all granted to you by Him ﷻ—so don't ever be too proud of yourself!

إِنَّهُۥ لَا يُحِبُّ ٱلْمُسْتَكْبِرِينَ

ʾInnahū lā yuḥibbu l-mustakbirīn

"He [Allāh ﷻ] does not like the arrogant."

— *Sūrat al-Naḥl (Qurʾān 16:23)*

Knowledge that does not make you humbler is a form of ignorance, just as status and wealth that don't make you more grateful to Allāh ﷻ are forms of corruption.

Someone who truly loves Allāh ﷻ and is grateful for His favor upon him cannot also be arrogant, because it is this love that takes one away from haughtiness and selfishness.

Aim to implant the love of Allāh ﷻ in your heart, as this will help you achieve humility and gain Allāh's love, ultimately opening the door to blessings and contentment.

إِنَّ ٱلصَّلَوٰةَ تَنْهَىٰ عَنِ ٱلْفَحْشَآءِ وَٱلْمُنكَرِ

ʾInna ṣ-ṣalāta tanhā ʿani l-faḥshāʾi wa-l-munkar

"Indeed, prayer prohibits immorality and wrongdoing."

— *Sūrat al-ʿAnkabūt (Qurʾān 29:45)*

The best way to reinforce your love for Allāh ﷻ, the love that makes one a better person, is through your adherence to the five prayers.

Prayer is an important appointment between you and the Creator—to always help you remember that He is near. Recite your words slowly and clearly to make sure that they are meaningful, and don't forget to supplicate during your prostrations for yourself and your loved ones.

After making such a beautiful and sincere connection with your Creator, would you allow yourself to engage in sinful acts?

Surely not, **as you and the devil will have taken completely different paths.**

وَلَا يَجْرِمَنَّكُمْ شَنَآنُ قَوْمٍ عَلَىٰٓ أَلَّا تَعْدِلُوا

Wa-lā yajrimannakum shanaʾānu qawmin
ʿalā ʾallā taʿdilū

"And do not let the hatred of a people prevent you from being just."

— *Sūrat al-Māʾidah (Qurʾān 5:8)*

You are going to encounter people in this life with whom you don't get along or share the same values or principles. Some of these people may even lie or cause trouble.

But you still have to be fair with them.

If you are a doctor or a nurse, you can't refuse to treat them.

If they are your employees, you might be able to take certain disciplinary measures that are allowed by law, but you can't withhold their rights from them.

Despite the frustrations that may come with this, cultivating a sense of justice in your character is indeed "nearer to righteousness [fearing Allāh ﷻ]."[15]

15. Qurʾān 5:8.

وَعَلَى ٱللَّهِ فَلْيَتَوَكَّلِ ٱلْمُؤْمِنُونَ

Wa-ʿalā llāhi fa-l-yatawakkali l-muʾminūn

"And upon Allāh let the believers rely."

— *Sūrat al-Māʾidah (Qurʾān 5:11)*

It doesn't matter how harsh your boss at work is...

Or how tough your exam will be...

Or how painful your medical treatment is...

Or how rude and unfeeling the people you depended on are.

Allāh ﷻ has appointed Himself as a Trustee and Disposer of your affairs.

So why the fear? The worries? The over-thinking?

"Whoever relies upon Allāh - then He is sufficient for him!"[16]

16. Qurʾān 65:3.

لَا تَدۡرِي لَعَلَّ ٱللَّهَ يُحۡدِثُ بَعۡدَ ذَٰلِكَ أَمۡرٗا

Lā tadrī la'alla llāha yuḥdithu ba'da dhālika 'amra

"You know not; perhaps Allāh will bring about after that a [different] matter."

— Sūrat al-Ṭalāq (Qur'ān 65:1)

Whenever you have a problem that creates difficulty for you in your personal or professional life...

Do not be so hasty about wanting to "solve" things that you end up losing everything important to you in the process.

If every student who faced difficulty with his or her studies dropped out, there would be no university graduates...

And if every disagreement between husbands and wives reached the point of irrevocable divorce, no families would remain intact.

A little wisdom, patience, and perseverance when handling such situations frequently leads to optimum results for everyone involved. By Allāh's will, a hard-working student who decides to keep going despite any obstacles can graduate and became successful at his or career, and a good marriage can be maintained when both parties understand what their priorities should be.

فَإِمْسَاكٌ بِمَعْرُوفٍ أَوْ تَسْرِيحٌ بِإِحْسَٰنٍ

Fa-ʾimsākun bi-maʿrūfin ʾaw tasrīḥun bi-ʾiḥsān

"Either keep [her] in an acceptable manner or release [her] with good treatment."

— *Sūrat al-Baqarah (Qurʾān 2:229)*

If divorce was inevitable despite your best efforts to save your marriage, don't be like those who break up in the worst way possible, as there can be no benefit in exchanging hurtful words or denying your spouse his or her rights. The same thing applies to a friendship that has come to an end for any reason.

Good treatment in such situations means respectful behavior and abiding by the limits set by Allāh ﷻ. It is also very important **not to speak badly about the other person or give away his or her secrets.**

If, on the other hand, things improved and you decided to give things a second chance, don't make your reconciliation a period of revenge and torture in which you keep reminding each other of your mistakes! In order for reconciliation to work, it should be a period of understanding and kindness.

وَلۡيَعۡفُواْ وَلۡيَصۡفَحُوٓاْۗ أَلَا تُحِبُّونَ أَن يَغۡفِرَ ٱللَّهُ لَكُمۡ

Wa-l-ya'fū wa-l-yaṣfaḥū 'a-lā tuḥibbūna
'an yaghfira llāhu lakum

"And let them pardon and overlook. Would you not like that Allāh should forgive you?"

—Sūrat al-Nūr (Qur'ān 24:22)

Be an easy-going person whom people always remember due to your kind and gentle nature.

Don't be too picky, and don't hold grudges. Be merciful in your dealings.

Forgiving others is the fastest way to gain Allāh's forgiveness.

"Be merciful on the earth, and you will be shown mercy from He Who is above the heavens."[17]

This is how it is when it comes to all of our interactions, whether we are dealing with people, or even plants or animals.

Remember that Allāh ﷻ will treat us the same way we have treated His creations.

17. *Jāmi' al-Tirmidhī, No. 1924.*

فَٱذۡكُرُونِيٓ أَذۡكُرۡكُمۡ

Fa-dhkurūnī ʾadhkurkum

"So remember Me; I will remember you."

— *Sūrat al-Baqarah (Qurʾān 2:152)*

If you wish to feel the love and blessings of Allāh ﷻ in your life...

And if you wish for Allāh ﷻ to answer your supplications...

Remember Him.

Whether you are sad, happy, or even angry...

Remember Him in every circumstance.

Otherwise, deliberately forgetting Him ﷻ and thus engaging in sinful acts with no regret or desire to repent means that one will never attain His blessings.

Work hard to follow His guidance, and do not allow anything to interfere.

وَسَارِعُوٓاْ إِلَىٰ مَغۡفِرَةٖ مِّن رَّبِّكُمۡ وَجَنَّةٍ عَرۡضُهَا ٱلسَّمَٰوَٰتُ
وَٱلۡأَرۡضُ أُعِدَّتۡ لِلۡمُتَّقِينَ

Wa-sāriʿū ʾilā maghfiratin min rabbikum wa-jannatin ʿarḍuhā s-samāwātu wa-l-ʾarḍu ʾuʿiddat li-l-muttaqīn

"And hasten to forgiveness from your Lord and a garden [i.e., Paradise] as wide as the heavens and earth, prepared for the righteous."

— *Sūrat Āli ʿImrān (Qurʾān 3:133)*

What are you waiting for? Why do you keep delaying seeking forgiveness from your Lord?

Is this temporary life worth more than Allāh's everlasting reward?

What more encouragement do you need?

The Lord Himself is telling you, "Hasten!"

This is probably the only act of haste that results in gain instead of waste!

Don't overthink the details; it is time to abandon your bad habits!

وَجَعَلَنِي مُبَارَكًا أَيْنَ مَا كُنتُ

Wa-jaʿalanī mubārakan ʾayna mā kunt

"And He has made me blessed wherever I am."

— *Sūrat Maryam (Qurʾān 19:31)*

Have you ever wondered what makes a person blessed?

Infinite possibilities come to mind.

For example, we might say that someone who lives a righteous life, is of benefit to his or her family, assists others whenever possible, and generally has a positive impact on the world is indeed blessed (by Allāh's will).

Or we might look to the words of Prophet Muḥammad ﷺ, who said:

"Whoever among you wakes up physically healthy, feeling safe and secure within himself, with food for the day, it is as if he acquired the whole world."[18]

Add to the above understandings of the word "blessed" with some of your own ideas, and then make this statement part of your daily supplications:

"O Allāh, make me blessed wherever I am."

The words are simple, but have great meaning.

18. *Sunan Ibn Mājah*, No. 4141.

لَا تَقْنَطُوا۟ مِن رَّحْمَةِ ٱللَّهِ

Lā taqnaṭū min raḥmati llāh

"Do not despair of the mercy of Allāh."

— *Sūrat al-Zumar (Qur'ān 39:53)*

If all the doors on this earth were to close, His door would remain open...

And if every promise ever made to you in your life was broken, Allāh ﷻ never fails in His promise.

He is the One who made the burning fire "coolness and safety upon Ibrāhīm (Abraham) [PBUH]."[19]

And He prevented a whole army from crushing an ant.[20]

He cured Prophet Ayyūb (Job) (PBUH) from a long and painful illness...

And He answered the prayer of Prophet Yūnus (Jonah) (PBUH) when he was enveloped in three layers of darkness—the darkness of the night, the darkness of the bottom of the sea, and the darkness of the fish's belly.

He is closer than we think, and much more merciful than we can comprehend.

19. Qur'ān 21:69.

20. Review Qur'ān 27:18-19.

ٱدۡعُونِيٓ أَسۡتَجِبۡ لَكُمۡ

Id'ūnī 'astajib lakum

"Call upon Me; I will respond to you."

— *Sūrat Ghāfir (Qur'ān 40:60)*

When you are distressed, call upon Him.

When you are uncertain, call upon Him.

When you feel powerless and defeated, call upon Him.

When you are in need, call upon Him.

When your sins burden you, call upon Him.

When you are happy, call upon Him.

Allāh ﷻ never tires of listening to His servants and answering their call—**and this is one of the clearest signs of His love for us.**

يُدَبِّرُ ٱلۡأَمۡرَ

Yudabbiru l-'amr

"He arranges [each] matter."

— Sūrat al-Sajdah (Qur'ān 32:5)

Sometimes strange things happen...

And things may not turn out the way we planned.

But when we look back, we realize that the things that happened were not, in fact, random.

Even if we don't understand the wisdom behind such things for a long time...

We eventually come to realize that they were all part of Allāh's plan for us—to guide us and anyone else who was present during each chapter of our lives.

Don't worry too much about how things are going to turn out.

Do your part, and leave the rest in the hands of He Who knows what is best for you and others.

وَٱللَّهُ أَعْلَمُ بِمَا وَضَعَتْ

Wa-llāhu 'a'lamu bi-mā waḍa'at

"And Allāh was most knowing of what she delivered."

— *Sūrat Āli 'Imrān (Qur'ān 3:36)*

When the pious wife of 'Imrān pledged to Allāh ﷻ that she would dedicate the contents of her womb entirely to His service at the sanctuary in Jerusalem, she didn't expect that she would give birth to a female, as it was only males who were known to perform this type of worship at the time.

Yet by Allāh's will, she gave birth to Maryam (AS), who indeed spent her life in the service of Allāh ﷻ and went on to become the mother of Prophet 'Īsá (Jesus) (PBUH).

You may sometimes assume that things have to turn out a certain way in order for other things to work out.

You may even mistakenly think that Allāh ﷻ did not answer your supplications when something turns out differently than what you initially imagined or planned.

Did the pious wife of 'Imrān take back her pledge once she had given birth to a female?

Absolutely not.

She instead trusted in Her Lord's plan and dedicated Maryam (AS) to His service, just as she had promised.

وَلَيْسَ ٱلذَّكَرُ كَٱلْأُنثَىٰ

Wa-laysa dh-dhakaru ka-l-ʾunthā

"And the male is not like the female."

— Sūrat Āli ʿImrān (Qurʾān 3:36)

The clear differences between the two genders were undoubtedly among the reasons why Allāh ﷻ willed for the pious wife of ʿImrān to give birth to a female instead of a male—a female who could bear the responsibility of being chosen above the women of the worlds to be the mother of Prophet ʿĪsá (Jesus) (PBUH).

By Allāh's will, ʿĪsá (PBUH) was placed in the care of a great woman.

Before this could happen, however, Maryam (AS) herself was placed in the care of a noble man—Prophet Zakariyyā (PBUH) —and this was also by Allāh's will.

Our differences can only make us great, because they allow us to support one other by doing the things we are best at within the capacities Allāh ﷻ created us with—and this is how great societies are built.

وَخَلَقْنَٰكُمْ أَزْوَٰجًا

Wa-khalaqnākum 'azwājā

"And We created you in pairs."

— *Sūrat al-Naba' (Qur'ān 78:8)*

The fact that each and every person on Earth was born to a pair, consisting of a male and a female, emphasizes **the great importance of both genders.**

It was never meant for us to live our lives in a perpetual "battle of the sexes," competing with the other gender to see which one brings more value to society.

We were created in pairs to complete one another—providing love and support to each other as we make our way through life.

"And of His signs is that He created for you from yourselves mates that you may find tranquility in them; and He placed between you affection and mercy. Indeed in that are signs for a people who give thought."[21]

21. Qur'ān 30:21.

لِيَتَّخِذَ بَعْضُهُم بَعْضًا سُخْرِيًّا

Li-yattakhidha baʿḍuhum baʿḍan sukhriyyā

"That they may make use of one another for service."

— *Sūrat al-Zukhruf (Qur'ān 43:32)*

Dear reader,

Have you ever wondered why Allāh ﷻ has blessed each one of us with different abilities and interests? This diversity is what allows us to be of service to each other and build stronger communities.

Here is a task for you related to the above verse:

Get a pen and a paper and write down some of your positive qualities along with the things that you love doing. What are you really good at? Also make note of any additional privileges you have been blessed with. For example, perhaps you have been blessed with extra wealth or are in a position to influence others with your ideas.

Then brainstorm ways of using these unique blessings and privileges to benefit others.

A personal example:

All thanks to Allāh ﷻ, I love reading the Qur'ān and researching the meaning of each verse.

I enjoy writing and sharing what I have learned with others...

And I am blessed by having connections with editors and publishers.

Thinking about the above helped me decide to write the book you are now holding between your hands, with the hope that it would help bring comfort to your heart and encourage you to read the Qur'ān with more understanding and awareness.

Now, what about you?

Don't delay your own creative ideas any further; it's time to start being of service to others today!

وَإِنِّي سَمَّيْتُهَا مَرْيَمَ

Wa-'innī sammaytuhā maryam

"And I have named her Maryam [Mary]."

— Sūrat Āli 'Imrān (Qur'ān 3:36)

Give your children beautiful, meaningful names rather than names that have questionable meanings or no meaning at all.

Trendy, exotic names have limited appeal, while the names of the prophets are timeless, as are the names of Prophet Muḥammad's wives, daughters, and Companions (may Allāh ﷻ be pleased with them all).

Make your children's names a pleasant Islamic experience that will always remind them of an Islamic figure, characteristic, quality, or something else that is pleasing to Allāh ﷻ. This is one of the rights they have over you as children.

وَإِنِّيٓ أُعِيذُهَا بِكَ وَذُرِّيَّتَهَا مِنَ ٱلشَّيۡطَٰنِ ٱلرَّجِيمِ

Wa-ʾinnī ʾuʿīdhuhā bika wa-dhurriyyatahā
mina sh-shayṭāni r-rajīm

"And I seek refuge for her in You and [for] her descendants from Satan, the accursed."

— *Sūrat Āli ʿImrān (Qurʾān 3:36)*

This how the pious wife of ʿImrān welcomed her newborn baby Maryam (AS) to this life, by making *duʿāʾ* for her and her future descendants.

Always make *duʿāʾ* for your sons and daughters, whether they are children or adults.

Pray for them, just as Maryam's mother prayed for her.

By Allāh's will and mercy, your sincere *duʿāʾ* may be the reason for their success in both this worldly life and in the Hereafter.

وَرَحْمَتِي وَسِعَتْ كُلَّ شَيْءٍ

Wa-raḥmatī wasiʿat kulla shayʾ

"My mercy encompasses all things."

— *Sūrat al-Aʿrāf (Qurʾān 7:156)*

The great mercy of our Creator can be spotted all around us if we just look.

It can be seen in the instincts He ﷻ put in animals to find the food they need to survive and not starve to death, and in the care mothers provide to their infants until they grow up and are able to take care of themselves.

It can be recognized in the way He ﷻ designed this earth, providing us with natural resources and making it bearable for us to live on.

It was by Allāh's mercy when you managed to start a career to support yourself and your family, and it was also by His mercy when you were granted unconditional love from the people closest to you.

What about that time when a kind friend comforted you with soothing words after you had a bad day?

And the fact that you have been able to overcome trauma from the past as you continue striving to do great things in life?

It was also by Allāh's mercy when that verse from the Qurʾān moved your heart.

But there is a special kind of mercy that is only granted to a specific category of people. Let us examine it in more detail in the next part of the verse quoted above...

سَأَكۡتُبُهَا لِلَّذِينَ يَتَّقُونَ وَيُؤۡتُونَ ٱلزَّكَوٰةَ وَٱلَّذِينَ هُم بِـَٔايَٰتِنَا يُؤۡمِنُونَ

Sa-ʾaktubuhā li-lladhīna yattaqūna wa-yuʾtūna
z-zakāta wa-lladhīna hum bi-ʾāyātinā yuʾminūn

"I will decree it [especially] for those who fear Me and give zakāh and those who believe in Our verses."

— *Sūrat al-Aʿrāf (Qurʾān 7:156)*

The privileged are those who actually recognize that it is Allāh's mercy that is sustaining their lives.

That's why they strive for even more of it with the knowledge that there is a special type of mercy reserved for those with true faith in Allāh ﷻ.

This is the mercy that strengthened the heart of the mother of Prophet Mūsá (Moses) (PBUH) when she had to cast Mūsá (PBUH) into the river while he was still a helpless infant.[22]

It is also the mercy that inspired Prophet Yaʿqūb (Jacob) (PBUH) to say, "Patience is most fitting—and Allāh [alone] is the One sought for help."[23]

This is the mercy that will allow one to enter Paradise.

O Allāh, let us be among those who strive harder!

22. Review Qurʾān 28:10.

23. Review Qurʾān 12:18.

إِنَّ ٱلدِّينَ عِندَ ٱللَّهِ ٱلْإِسْلَٰمُ

ʾInna d-dīna ʿinda llāhi l-ʾislām

"Indeed, the religion in the sight of Allāh is Islām."

— *Sūrat Āli ʿImrān (Qurʾān 3:19)*

Islām is not the same as Christianity, Judaism, or Buddhism.

Yes, all religions on Earth contain beautiful teachings that encourage love, tolerance, and self-discipline.

But it's important to understand that the only religion revealed by Allāh ﷻ that is also free of corruption is Islām, and this has always been the case, even before the prophethood of Prophet Muḥammad ﷺ.

ʿĪsá (Jesus), Mūsá (Moses), and Ibrāhīm (Abraham) (PBUT) were all Muslims.

But it was people who corrupted their teachings, eventually turning them into different religions.

Even today, we see people who interpret the teachings of Islām according to their own desires, picking and choosing what to follow, and attempting to mislead others in the process.

Yet the difference is that they **cannot ever distort or tamper with Allāh's clear words in the Qurʾān**, because Allāh ﷻ Himself promised that these scriptures will remain preserved until the end of time.

As such, Islām is the last of the heavenly revealed religions.

To those who have doubts about the true religion they should follow:

Read the Qur'ān, and be honest with your Creator before anyone else.

وَوَجَدَكَ ضَآلًّا فَهَدَىٰ

Wa-wajadaka ḍāllan fa-hadā

"And He found you lost and guided [you]."

— Sūrat al-Ḍuḥá (Qur'ān 93:7)

Do you remember that person who was constantly reminding you to pray?

And that day when you woke up just in time for Fajr prayer?

What about that verse from the Qur'ān that suddenly appeared on the screen and spoke right to your heart while you were scrolling through social media?

Or that time you felt guilty because you knew deep inside that your behavior should have been more pleasing to Allāh ﷻ?

Were these all random occurrences?

No, they are part of Allāh's daily guidance to all of us...

Because He wants us to take the right path...

And have hearts full of tranquility despite the harshness of the road.

This is just a small part of the love He continuously shows to us.

فَإِنۡ أَسۡلَمُواْ فَقَدِ ٱهۡتَدَواْ

Fa-ʾin ʾaslamū fa-qadi htadaw

"And if they submit [in Islām], they are rightly guided."

— *Sūrat Āli ʿImrān (Qurʾān 3:20)*

He made the road easy for you to be guided.

Every new turn contains visible signs and reminders right before your eyes.

But do you submit?

Or do you turn away in annoyance?

It's not enough to claim, "I am a believer."

It's not enough to say, "I am a Muslim."

Do you submit?

To every single word revealed in the Qurʾān?

Do you apply the teachings of Islām to your life?

Ask yourself these questions the next time you are at a crossroad.

فَفِرُّوٓا۟ إِلَى ٱللَّهِ

Fa-firrū ʾilā llāh

"So flee to Allāh."

— *Sūrat al-Dhāriyāt (Qur'ān 51:50)*

Just like a child who seeks his mother's embrace for comfort after a nightmare...

Seek refuge in Allāh ﷻ...

From bad things that destroy the soul...

From evil people...

From bad thoughts that plague your mind...

From negative thinking...

From doubts...

From life's difficult situations...

From your sins...

And much more.

Turn to Him.

Don't be hesitant or afraid that He won't accept you.

He is more kind to His servants than a mother is to her child.[24]

24. Based on a saying of Prophet Muḥammad ﷺ (review *Ṣaḥiḥ Muslim*, No. 2754).

أَلَيْسَ ذَٰلِكَ بِقَٰدِرٍ عَلَىٰٓ أَن يُحْـِۧيَ ٱلْمَوْتَىٰ

ʾA-laysa dhālika bi-qādirin ʿalā ʾan yuḥyiya l-mawtā

"Is not that [Creator] Able to give life to the dead?"

— *Sūrat al-Qiyāmah (Qurʾān 75:40)*

My friend,

Don't be afraid of any doubts or questions that may occur to you regarding the unseen.

Don't hate yourself or think that you are committing a big sin by having such thoughts.

Allāh ﷻ is aware of our doubts and other feelings; He is the Creator of humankind and knows exactly how we think!

This is why the Qurʾān provides us with many examples of things we are familiar with in this worldly life—so that we may build faith as we recognize and contemplate the vastness of His creation.

Look at how He created us after we were nothing...

And how He gives life to the earth after its lifelessness...

And how He organized every single thing in this universe to make life possible for us.

"We have made clear to you the signs; perhaps you will understand."[25]

25. Qurʾān 57:17.

فَٱصۡبِرۡ إِنَّ وَعۡدَ ٱللَّهِ حَقٌّ

Fa-ṣbir ʾinna waʿda llāhi ḥaqq

"So be patient. Indeed, the promise of Allāh is truth."

— *Sūrat al-Rūm (Qurʾān 30:60)*

Don't let prolonged negative situations make you lose hope in Allāh's promises.

Prophet Yaʿqūb (Jacob) (PBUH) had to wait for a long number of very difficult years before he could be reunited again with his beloved son Yūsuf (Joseph) (PBUH), yet he kept saying: "Indeed, no one despairs of relief from Allāh except the disbelieving people."[26]

Prophet Muḥammad ﷺ and his Companions (may Allāh be pleased with them all) had to endure twenty-one years of hardship and persecution before they could finally liberate Makkah from the evils of idol-worship.

And the pious wife of Firʿawn had no doubt that Allāh ﷻ would save her,[27] even though she was trapped with the most oppressive ruler of that era.

The believers are the ones who will be saved...

26. Qurʾān 12:87.

27. Review Qurʾān 66:11.

And His light is what will prevail.

All rights will be returned to their owners...

And the believers will be rewarded while the wrongdoers will be punished.

Have patience.

وُجُوهٌ يَوْمَئِذٍ نَّاضِرَةٌ إِلَىٰ رَبِّهَا نَاظِرَةٌ

Wujūhun yawma'idhin nāḍirah
'ilā rabbihā nāẓirah

"[Some] faces, that Day, will be radiant, looking at their Lord."

—*Sūrat al-Qiyāmah (Qur'ān 75:22–23)*

You would really like to see Him, right?

This is about your Lord, the One Who has been kind and merciful to you all throughout the long journey of your life...

The One Who has saved you numerous times and blessed you with countless blessings...

The One Who listens to your worries and always comforts your soul when you turn to Him...

The One Who did not leave you lost even when you ignored His guidance and went astray...

The One Who loves you more than anyone in this world.

Place these verses where you can always look at them as a reminder for you to remain a good Muslim.

You wouldn't want to miss the great privilege of finally being able to see Him, would you?

وَقُولُواْ لِلنَّاسِ حُسْنًا

Wa-qūlū li-n-nāsi ḥusnā

"And speak to people good [words]."

—Sūrat al-Baqarah (Qur'ān 2:83)

Before you say anything to anyone, remember that Allāh ﷻ loves gentleness and does not approve of rudeness or harshness in speech.

Let "peace be upon you" (*as-salāmu 'alaykum*) be the first words you say whenever you start a conversation with someone.

Being in a bad mood is not an excuse for hurting others.

Don't be the reason for someone's tears, self-doubt, or heartbreak.

Represent Islām in your speech.

وَعَاشِرُوهُنَّ بِٱلْمَعْرُوفِ

Wa-ʿāshirūhunna bi-l-maʿrūf

"And live with them in kindness."

— *Sūrat al-Nisāʾ (Qurʾān 4:19)*

To every man who has a wife:

Let the best of all men, Prophet Muḥammad ﷺ, be your role model on how to live with your wife in kindness.

- Consult with her and show that you value her advice, like the Prophet ﷺ valued the advice of his wise wife Umm Salamah (RA), who played an important role in counselling the Prophet ﷺ.
- Don't burden her with unreasonable or excessive requests, and help her when you are able to do so, as the Prophet ﷺ used to mend his clothes by himself and help at home as much as he could.
- Engage with her in fun activities, like the Prophet ﷺ frequently did with ʿĀʾishah (RA) in particular (due to her young age), speaking to her in a playful manner and even racing her. He also used to walk with her during the evening as they chatted about various things.
- Declare how proud you are of her, like the Prophet ﷺ used to praise Khadījah (RA) for her many excellent qualities.

وَقَدْ خَابَ مَنْ حَمَلَ ظُلْمًا

Wa-qad khāba man ḥamala ẓulmā

"And he will have failed who carries injustice."

— *Sūrat Ṭā-Hā (Qur'ān 20:111)*

To be just, we should continually assess how we treat the people around us, whether at home or elsewhere.

A husband should make sure to give his wife all of her rights, just as a wife should be respectful to her husband and the other members of her household.

A manager must be fair with his or her employees, just as an employee must work honestly and sincerely.

Parents should take care of their children's needs, just as adult men and women should also take care of the needs of their elderly parents.

Do you work to improve your treatment of others and compensate for your shortcomings?

وَلَا تَمْشِ فِي ٱلْأَرْضِ مَرَحًا

Wa-lā tamshi fī l-ʾarḍi maraḥā

"And do not walk upon the earth exultantly."

— *Sūrat al-Isrāʾ (Qurʾān 17:37)*

Despite our different abilities and statuses in this worldly life, Allāh ﷻ has made us equal in one important respect—that we have all been "created weak,"[28] making each and every single one of us "in need of Allāh."[29]

We all get sick...

We all feel sad...

And no one can escape death.

It is He alone ﷻ Who made it possible for us to achieve whatever we have achieved in life, and the same blessings we often take for granted can all be gone in the blink of an eye.

Being aware of this makes us much humbler when celebrating our worldly achievements.

It makes us kinder and more merciful toward others.

It also suppresses the envy in our hearts, which is the best state one could ever reach.

28. Qurʾān 4:28.

29. Qurʾān 35:15.

ٱدْعُ إِلَىٰ سَبِيلِ رَبِّكَ بِٱلْحِكْمَةِ وَٱلْمَوْعِظَةِ ٱلْحَسَنَةِ

Udʿu ʾilā sabīli rabbika bi-l-ḥikmati
wa-l-mawʿiẓati l-ḥasanah

"Invite to the way of your Lord with wisdom and good instruction."

— *Sūrat al-Naḥl (Qurʾān 16:125)*

Have you paid attention to how Allāh ﷻ conveys His message to us in the Qurʾān?

Not only do the verses contain many parables to aid understanding, but He ﷻ also constantly reminds us of what is good for us, using logic that appeals to the human mind, and showing us that any bad we do is a transgression against our own selves and others. We learn that our Merciful and Forgiving Creator is al-Tawwāb ("The Accepting of Repentance") (providing us with continuous motivation to repent), yet we also learn that He is "severe in penalty" for those who persist in sin.[30]

If the Lord of the Worlds has taken this fair and loving approach in delivering His message to us, would it make any sense if Prophet Muḥammad ﷺ had been harsh in his preaching?

What about us? Would it make any sense to adopt an approach that Allāh ﷻ and His Messenger ﷺ did not take?

30. Review Qurʾān 5:98.

Before you give Islamic advice to someone, make sure that you are giving it purely for the sake of Allāh ﷻ. Following the authentic *sunnah* of the Prophet ﷺ means that you offer advice because you wish goodness for the person, and not because you feel superior to the person you are advising.

Remember: We all have shortcomings.

إِنَّ ٱلْحَسَنَٰتِ يُذْهِبْنَ ٱلسَّيِّـَٔاتِ

ʾInna l-ḥasanāti yudhhibna s-sayyiʾāt

"Indeed, good deeds do away with misdeeds."

— *Sūrat Hūd (Qurʾān 11:114)*

Don't suppress the goodness in your heart thinking that you are unworthy because of any sins you may have committed in the past.

As a believer, you are constantly washing away your sins without even realizing it.

Don't underestimate:

- The help you provide to your family;
- The smile on your face;
- The good words you have uttered;
- Any acts of Islamic worship that you regularly perform.

You may forget the good you have done, but He won't.

إِنَّهُمْ كَانُوا۟ يُسَٰرِعُونَ فِى ٱلْخَيْرَٰتِ وَيَدْعُونَنَا رَغَبًا وَرَهَبًا
وَكَانُوا۟ لَنَا خَٰشِعِينَ

ʾInnahum kānū yusāriʿūna fī l-khayrāti
wa-yadʿūnanā raghaban wa-rahaban wa-kānū
lanā khāshiʿīn

"Indeed, they used to hasten to good deeds and supplicate Us in hope and fear, and they were to Us humbly submissive."

— *Sūrat al-Anbiyāʾ (Qurʾān 21:90)*

When reading this verse in context you will notice that it is a description of the prophets mentioned in the verses prior to this (in the same chapter).[31]

One of the main things these prophets had in common is that Allāh ﷻ answered their supplications, favored them above others, and removed their hardships, which tells us that **this verse actually contains the secret to having your supplications answered!**

Your good deeds and sincere submission to Allāh ﷻ do much more than wash away your sins; they may also be the reason why Allāh ﷻ answers the supplications that you keep making day after day and night after night without despair of His mercy—and this is one of the greatest rewards granted to the righteous in this worldly life.

31. Review Qurʾān 21:48–90.

فَوَسۡوَسَ لَهُمَا ٱلشَّيۡطَٰنُ لِيُبۡدِيَ لَهُمَا مَا وُۥرِيَ عَنۡهُمَا مِن سَوۡءَٰتِهِمَا

Fa-waswasa lahumā sh-shayṭānu li-yubdiya lahumā mā wūriya ʿanhumā min sawʾātihimā

"But Satan whispered to them to make apparent to them that which was concealed from them of their nakedness."

— *Sūrat al-Aʿrāf (Qurʾān 7:20)*

Of course, Satan did not inform Ādam (PBUH) and his wife of his true intentions; he instead deceived them into thinking that they would become angels or attain immortality if they ate from the fruits of the tree that had been forbidden to them. He even swore by Allāh that he was among their sincere advisors.[32]

But the thing is, Allāh ﷻ had already told them not to come close to that tree![33]

When you know that something has been forbidden by Allāh ﷻ, don't try to bypass His prohibitions and then blame the circumstance!

Ādam (PBUH) and his wife immediately realized that they had wronged themselves and tried to cover themselves with the

32. Review Qurʾān 7:20–21.

33. Qurʾān 7:19.

leaves of Paradise as they asked Allāh ﷻ to forgive them and have mercy upon them.

What about me, you, and every single one of us? Do we have enough self-awareness to recognize the times when we are not fully obedient to Allāh ﷻ? And if we have committed a sin, do we persist in our sin and allow Satan to achieve his goal of harming us?

Or do we humble ourselves by abandoning the sin and following Allāh's commandments instead?

وَلِبَاسُ ٱلتَّقْوَىٰ ذَٰلِكَ خَيْرٌ

Wa-libāsu t-taqwā dhālika khayr

"But the clothing of righteousness - that is best."

— *Sūrat al-Aʿrāf (Qurʾān 7:26)*

Just as clothing is meant to conceal a person's nakedness and provide him or her with adornment as a means of honoring humankind, a believer should also strive to suppress any negative personal traits by engaging in acts that add "beauty" to one's character, which is what happens when we embody good Islamic morals, including modesty in our dress, speech, and behavior.

One who succeeds at this effectively dons the "clothing of righteousness" **in which true freedom is found**, unlike the many misconceptions of "freedom" present in today's society that call for all forms of depravity, putting many on an evil path that will eventually corrupt and destroy their innate sense of right and wrong when immorality becomes normalized.

فَلَا تَغُرَّنَّكُمُ ٱلْحَيَوٰةُ ٱلدُّنْيَا

Fa-lā taghurrannakumu l-ḥayātu d-dunyā

"So let not the worldly life delude you."

— *Sūrat Fāṭir (Qur'ān 35:5)*

If you don't want this worldly life to delude you, **maintain your devotion to the five obligatory prayers.**

They are your shield from the temptations of this worldly life and serve as a constant reminder of the Hereafter.

Allāh ﷻ teaches us that prayer is an essential act of worship that a Muslim must never abandon regardless of the circumstance.

Even in times of danger or battle, the early Muslims were not exempted from prayer, and were taught by Allāh ﷻ to pray *Ṣalāt al-Khawf* ("The Prayer of Fear").[34]

34. Review Qur'ān 2:239 and 4:102.

قُلْ مَنْ حَرَّمَ زِينَةَ ٱللَّهِ ٱلَّتِيٓ أَخْرَجَ لِعِبَادِهِۦ

Qul man ḥarrama zīnata llāhi llatī 'akhraja li-'ibādih

"Say, 'Who has forbidden the adornment of [i.e., from] Allāh which He has produced for His servants.'"

— Sūrat al-A'rāf (Qur'ān 7:32)

It is true one must be cautious about falling into worldly temptations.

But this great verse tells us that the "adornments" of this life were, in fact, produced for the believers to enjoy and benefit from in this worldly life, and will be exclusively theirs on the Day of Resurrection,[35] while the corrupt will have no share in them anymore once they have failed the tests of this worldly life.

Enjoying the lawful provisions we are blessed with in this world can be a form of worship if we also show gratitude to Allāh ﷻ and do not become greedy or selfish, withholding our blessings from others. We should also **remember to exercise moderation**, as Allāh ﷻ tells us: "Eat and drink, but be not excessive. Indeed, He likes not those who commit excess."[36]

35. Qur'ān 7:32.

36. Qur'ān 7:31.

قَالَتْ هُوَ مِنْ عِندِ ٱللَّهِ

Qālat huwa min ʿindi llāh

"She said, 'It is from Allāh.'"

— *Sūrat Āli ʿImrān (Qurʾān 3:37)*

Whenever Prophet Zakariyyā (PBUH) entered the sanctuary to see Maryam (AS), he would find that she always had food despite her being alone in the prayer chamber, causing him to ask: "O Maryam, from where is this [coming] to you?"[37]

"It is from Allāh," she told him. "Indeed, Allāh provides for whom He wills without account."[38]

The food you have on your table is from Allāh ﷻ.

The bed you sleep on is from Allāh ﷻ.

Your sight, your hearing, and even your ability to think critically are all provisions from Allāh ﷻ.

Taking these blessings for granted may make you forget this, so thank Allāh ﷻ every day for all that you have been blessed with.

37. Qurʾān 3:37.

38. Qurʾān 3:37.

هُنَالِكَ دَعَا زَكَرِيَّا رَبَّهُۥ

Hunālika da'ā zakariyyā rabbah

"At that, Zakariyyā called upon his Lord."

— *Sūrat Āli 'Imrān (Qur'ān 3:38)*

After Maryam's touching words about Allāh's care for her in the prayer chamber, Zakariyyā (PBUH) was inspired to make *du'ā'* to Allāh ﷻ in the very same spot, knowing that our Creator ﷻ is Most Generous with His faithful servants.

Despite his old age and the fact that his wife was barren, Zakariyyā (PBUH) asked Allāh ﷻ to grant him the bounty of righteous offspring, saying: "Indeed, You are the Hearer of [All] Prayers."[39]

While making this supplication, he also said: "Never have I been in my supplication to You, my Lord, unhappy [i.e., disappointed]."[40]

From this story, one can learn the art of feeling genuinely happy for others.

When you see that someone is blessed, don't go wishing for the person to lose his or her blessings, like some unbelieving people do—sometimes going even further to harm the person in question.

39. Qur'ān 3:38.

40. Qur'ān 19:4.

The One Who blessed that person can bless you the same way—or even more, according to His will!

Wish good for the person, and ask Allāh ﷻ to be generous with you like He was generous to others.

Never forget that it is Allāh ﷻ Who provides for all of His creations!

وَٱللَّهُ خَيْرُ ٱلرَّٰزِقِينَ

Wa-llāhu khayru r-rāziqīn

"And Allāh is the best of providers."

— Sūrat al-Jumuʿah (Qurʾān 62:11)

We must not let the ease of committing *ḥarām* (prohibited) acts deceive us into thinking that such acts are the only guaranteed means of obtaining what one wants.

Striving hard in this life and always choosing *ḥalāl* over *ḥarām* means that you trust in His wisdom in planning your affairs, and that you have confidence in the fact that whatever Allāh ﷻ has willed for you will definitely come to pass, despite any difficulties or interference from others.

Whether it's material wealth, health, safety, contentment, a righteous spouse, or having your supplications answered...

These are all provisions from Allāh ﷻ.

O Allāh, provide us with what is best for us, and let us not be in need of anyone except for You.

وَلَمَّا بَلَغَ أَشُدَّهُۥ وَٱسْتَوَىٰٓ ءَاتَيْنَٰهُ حُكْمًا وَعِلْمًا

Wa-lammā balagha ʾashuddahū wa-stawā
ʾātaynāhu ḥukman wa-ʿilmā

"And when he attained his full strength and was [mentally] mature, We bestowed upon him judgement and knowledge."

—Sūrat al-Qaṣaṣ (Qurʾān 28:14)

One often has to go through different stages of both mental and physical growth before Allāh ﷻ grants him His provision.

It is during these times that one must work hard so that patience can be learned and fear can be overcome.

We see this clearly in the story of Mūsá (PBUH).

Allāh ﷻ gave him many provisions, each one at the right time and place.

Meanwhile, during each stage of his life (even prior to his prophethood), Mūsá (PBUH) would do a good deed and supplicate to Allāh ﷻ before receiving the reward of provision.

Allāh ﷻ tells us: **"And thus do We reward the doers of good."**[41]

41. Qurʾān 28:14.

رَبِّ إِنِّي لِمَآ أَنزَلۡتَ إِلَيَّ مِنۡ خَيۡرٍ فَقِيرٌ

Rabbi ʾinnī li-mā ʾanzalta ʾilayya min khayrin faqīr

"My Lord, indeed I am, for whatever good You would send down to me, in need."

—Sūrat al-Qaṣaṣ (Qur'ān 28:24)

This supplication made by Prophet Mūsá (PBUH) is one of the best and most humble supplications one could ever make to Allāh ﷻ.

Someone who says these words is basically acknowledging his or her complete trust in Allāh ﷻ while also expressing satisfaction and contentment with the outcome. This is what happens when you submit to His will and hand your affairs over to Him alone.

Make this *du'ā'* one of your daily supplications, and **look forward to the good that Allāh ﷻ will bless you with every single day (by His will and mercy).**

يَٰٓأَبَتِ ٱسْتَـْٔجِرْهُ

Yā-ʾabati staʾjirh

"O my father, hire him."

—*Sūrat al-Qaṣaṣ (Qurʾān 28:26)*

"Allāh helps His servant so long as he helps his brother."[42]

In a land called Madyan that was foreign to him, Mūsá (PBUH) encountered two women near a crowded well who wanted to help their elderly father by fetching water for his flocks. Out of modesty, however, they were waiting until the male shepherds in the area finished their business there.

Without hesitation, Mūsá (PBUH) fetched water for them and did not ask for anything in return.

The two women were extremely grateful for Mūsá's help and told their father what had transpired, so he invited him to his home to thank him, and one of his daughters suggested that they hire him.

Because Mūsá (PBUH) helped these people, he was in turn recognized by them for his goodness, strength, and trustworthiness.[43] He was also granted a safe place to stay with a good family, and provided with a job, and even a wife when he married one of the two women.

42. *The Comprehensive Book of Ḥadīth (Book 16, Ḥadīth No. 29).*

43. Refer to the same verse (Qurʾān 28:26).

The good you do for people that is purely for the sake of Allāh ﷻ can only bring you good in return, and this is also true of the good you do for yourself, as it often leads you to good places along the way.

إِنِّيٓ أَخَافُ أَن يُكَذِّبُونِ

ʾInnī ʾakhāfu ʾan yukadhdhibūn

"I fear that they will deny me."

— *Sūrat al-Shuʿarāʾ (Qurʾān 26:12)*

Whenever someone steps out of his or her comfort zone, it is only natural for that person to express worry and fear.

This was certainly the case with Mūsá (PBUH).

Being sent once again to the land of the oppressive Firʿawn after he had been away for many years (this time to deliver the message of Allāh ﷻ) was undoubtedly a very difficult mission for Mūsá (PBUH) to undertake.

Just as anyone may experience tension prior to a new and challenging phase, Mūsá (PBUH) expressed anxiety about the situation, saying that he feared several things—that his breast would tighten, that his tongue would not be fluent, and that he would be killed.[44]

Yet he did not run away from his mission; he instead asked Allāh ﷻ to help him and make matters easy for him.

In response, Allāh ﷻ answered Mūsá's supplication, sending his brother Hārūn (Aaron) (PBUH) with him for support.

44. Review Qurʾān 26:13–14.

Each new chapter in our lives contains elements of the unknown, which may cause some distress, even when the changes are supposed to be positive ones.

So, remember the example of Mūsá (PBUH), and have faith that **Allāh ﷻ always sends help and ease along the way to assist us in achieving our individual missions on Earth.**

كَلَّآ إِنَّ مَعِيَ رَبِّي سَيَهۡدِينِ

Kallā ʾinna maʿiya rabbī sa-yahdīn

"No! Indeed, with me is my Lord; He will guide me."

—*Sūrat al-Shuʿarāʾ (Qurʾān 26:62)*

O Allāh, grant us the tranquility of Mūsá (PBUH).

Years after Mūsá's prophethood, he and the other believers had to leave the land of oppression when Firʿawn became extreme in his injustice, making the situation unbearable.

But when they fled, Firʿawn and his soldiers pursued them.

As fear overwhelmed Mūsá's companions, they said: "Indeed, we are to be overtaken!"[45]

But Mūsá (PBUH) remained steadfast and said: **"No! Indeed, with me is my Lord; He will guide me."**[46]

He did not express fear as he had in the earlier stages of his prophethood, as experience taught him that Allāh ﷻ is more powerful than any circumstance, and that He always saves the believers.

Reflect on this story, and don't hesitate to fulfill your own mission in life. No circumstance is too great when Allāh ﷻ is by your side.

45. Qurʾān 26:61.

46. Qurʾān 26:62.

فَإِنَّ مَعَ ٱلْعُسْرِ يُسْرًا

Fa-ʾinna maʿa l-ʿusri yusrā

"For indeed, with hardship [will be] ease [i.e., relief]."

— *Sūrat al-Sharḥ (Qur'ān 94:5)*

Allāh ﷻ confirms this twice in a row, as the same phrase is repeated in the verse that follows the one quoted above.[47]

Note that Allāh ﷻ did not say that ease comes "after" hardship; He said that ease comes "**with**" hardship. Scholars have explained that the grammar of the Arabic verse also makes it clear that every hardship that a person may experience comes with unlimited ease.

So, **do not grieve.**

This is the message Allāh ﷻ conveyed to Maryam (AS) when she experienced the pain of childbirth and found herself faced with big new responsibilities.[48]

He ﷻ also conveyed these words to the mother of Prophet Mūsá (PBUH) when she had to cast Mūsá (PBUH) into the river while he was still a newborn infant.[49]

And He ﷻ once again conveyed the same message to Prophet Muḥammad ﷺ and his noble Companions (may Allāh be

47. Review Qur'ān 94:6.

48. Qur'ān 19:24.

49. Qur'ān 28:7.

pleased with them all) after they had lost to the non-believers in the Battle of Uḥud.[50]

These situations were indeed full of hardship, but immense blessings and relief came with them as well.

Take it easy.

50. Qur'ān 3:139.

فَاللَّهُ خَيْرٌ حَٰفِظًا

Fa-llāhu khayrun ḥāfiẓā

"Allāh is the best guardian."

— *Sūrat Yūsuf (Qur'ān 12:64)*

Say it to yourself, and be conscious of the meaning...

Whenever you feel worry or tension in your heart...

Whenever you are traveling...

Whenever you encounter a stressful situation...

Whenever things at work don't go the way you planned...

And it **shall bound fast your heart**, *in shā' Allāh.*

قَالَ لَا تَخَافَآ إِنَّنِي مَعَكُمَآ أَسْمَعُ وَأَرَىٰ

Qāla lā takhāfā ʾinnanī maʿakumā ʾasmaʿu wa-ʾarā

"[Allāh] said, 'Fear not. Indeed, I am with you both; I hear and I see.'"

— *Sūrat Ṭā-Hā (Qurʾān 20:46)*

Know that you can face anything and anyone so long as you are aiming for goodness.

No one can hurt you regardless of their attempts; The Most Powerful is by your side!

Don't let your mind deceive you into thinking you are alone.

Even if everyone you know abandoned or forgot you...

Your Lord is never forgetful.

Trust in Him.

وَإِذَا مَرِضْتُ فَهُوَ يَشْفِينِ

Wa-'idhā mariḍtu fa-huwa yashfīn

"And when I am ill, it is He who cures me."

—Sūrat al-Shu'arā' (Qur'ān 26:80)

As distressing as tough situations are, they teach one to become more humble to Allāh ﷻ.

If you ever suffer from mental or physical illness, remember that it is only Allāh ﷻ Who can help you get better.

Medications may be part of the help that He willed for us to have (and we should take them when needed), but we still depend on the Most Merciful Creator for complete relief from the things that ail us.

Whenever you are ill, recite this supplication taught to us by Ayyūb (Job) (PBUH): **"Indeed, adversity has touched me, and You are the most merciful of the merciful."**[51]

51. Qur'ān 21:83.

إِنَّا لِلَّهِ وَإِنَّآ إِلَيْهِ رَٰجِعُونَ

ʾInnā li-llāhi wa-ʾinnā ʾilayhi rājiʿūn

"Indeed we belong to Allāh, and indeed to Him we will return."

— *Sūrat al-Baqarah (Qurʾān 2:156)*

As Muslims, we frequently say this statement in response to the news of someone's death or another calamity.

But have you ever thought more deeply about the meaning of the words?

As independent as we try to be, we do not actually belong to ourselves! Nor do we belong to this world!

When we finally realize this, we will find that it's not worth devastating ourselves over worldly matters.

Act as a faithful servant of Allāh ﷻ during your limited time on Earth, and be patient.

Allāh ﷻ says that the patient ones who realize this ultimate truth are "the ones upon whom are blessings from their Lord and mercy. And it is those who are the [rightly] guided."[52]

52. Qurʾān 2:157.

وَكُلُّهُمْ ءَاتِيهِ يَوْمَ ٱلْقِيَٰمَةِ فَرْدًا

Wa-kulluhum ʾātīhi yawma l-qiyāmati fardā

"And all of them are coming to Him on the Day of Resurrection alone."

— Sūrat Maryam (Qurʾān 19:95)

Dear self,

You will come to Him alone...

Not with your friends, not with your parents, not with your spouse or even your children...

Not with your money, not with your status...

Not with your everyday masks.

It will be your naked self alone, in front of Him.

Are you ready for this?

Do you work hard enough on purifying your intentions and deeds alike?

Strive to perform a secret act of worship known only to Allāh ﷻ that shall make you feel content on the Day when you finally meet Him, *in shāʾ Allāh*.

فَلَا تَعْلَمُ نَفْسٌ مَّآ أُخْفِيَ لَهُم مِّن قُرَّةِ أَعْيُنٍ جَزَآءًۢ بِمَا كَانُوا۟ يَعْمَلُونَ

Fa-lā taʿlamu nafsun mā ʾukhfiya lahum min qurrati ʾaʿyunin jazāʾan bi-mā kānū yaʿmalūn

"And no soul knows what has been hidden for them of comfort for eyes [i.e., satisfaction] as reward for what they used to do."

— *Sūrat al-Sajdah (Qurʾān 32:17)*

As indicated in the Qurʾān and the authentic *sunnah* of Prophet Muḥammad ﷺ, there are certain acts of worship that bring one closer to the Creator, including the following:

- Charity given so secretly that even your left hand does not know what your right hand has given;
- Night prayer;
- Supplication;
- Things done to alleviate the suffering of others;
- Fasting.

When performed in secret, these acts will remain something known only to you and Allāh ﷻ, providing you with even greater closeness and rewards in the Hereafter.

Aim to be from among those who truly love Allāh ﷻ, and **not among those who instead commit sins in secret.**

وَوَجَدُوا۟ مَا عَمِلُوا۟ حَاضِرًا وَلَا يَظْلِمُ رَبُّكَ أَحَدًا

Wa-wajadū mā ʿamilū ḥāḍiran wa-lā yaẓlimu rabbuka ʾaḥada

"And they will find what they did present [before them]. And your Lord does injustice to no one."

— *Sūrat al-Kahf (Qurʾān 18:49)*

You hate it, right? It feels really bad when someone continuously reminds you of your past mistakes, flaws, and shortcomings.

On the other hand, you surely feel very happy when people remember all of the good you have done and express love and gratitude toward you.

Remember that Allāh ﷻ has a full record of our deeds in His possession. Everything we have ever done, good and bad, is recorded there, including even the tiniest of deeds.

While this may be unsettling to think about when we recall our past mistakes, remember that this record also contains evidence of our sincere repentance, our truthful tears shed in remembrance of Him ﷻ, our attempts at reforming ourselves for the better, and our secret acts of worship.

Beware of what you say and do in this worldly life so that the moment when your book of recorded deeds is opened in front of you on the Day of Judgment is not one of sadness and regret.

And remember...

Each and every minute that we are alive presents a fresh opportunity to do good deeds and repent from our sins!

يَقُولُ يَٰلَيْتَنِي قَدَّمْتُ لِحَيَاتِي

Yaqūlu yā-laytanī qaddamtu li-ḥayātī

"He will say, 'Oh, I wish I had sent ahead [some good] for my life.'"

— *Sūrat al-Fajr (Qur'ān 89:24)*

This will be the state of those who did not work for their Hereafter.

Starting from today, let us make it a goal to renew our intentions so that even our everyday routines in this life are purely for the sake of Allāh ﷻ.

For example, if you are responsible for cooking for your family, do it with the intention of bringing happiness to their hearts.

Make the time you spend with your loved ones an act of goodness to them, as Allāh ﷻ has asked of us.[53]

Do not say anything unless you have something good to say.

Sleep with the intention of waking up the next morning to pray Fajr in order to start the new day by pleasing Allāh ﷻ.

These are indeed simple things, but they are actually what **build the foundations for our homes in Paradise,** ***in shā' Allāh.***

53. Qur'ān 4:36.

وَلَا تَقُولَنَّ لِشَاْيْءٍ إِنِّي فَاعِلٌ ذَٰلِكَ غَدًا إِلَّآ أَن يَشَآءَ ٱللَّهُ

Wa-lā taqūlanna li-shay'in 'innī fā'ilun dhālika ghadan 'illā 'an yashā'a llāh

"And never say of anything, 'Indeed, I will do that tomorrow,' except [when adding], 'If Allāh wills.'"

— *Sūrat al-Kahf (Qur'ān 18:23–24)*

This is a reminder to ask Allāh ﷻ for His help with each step that we take in life. If our plans are what is best for us, *O Allāh make them work—and if not, please guide us to something better.*

Don't be too attached to your plans when they appear to go in a different direction than what you originally had in mind.

Above all, **trust in Allāh's wisdom.**

لَا تَحْسَبُوهُ شَرًّا لَّكُم بَلْ هُوَ خَيْرٌ لَّكُمْ

Lā taḥsabūhu sharran lakum bal huwa khayrun lakum

"Do not think it bad for you; rather, it is good for you."

— Sūrat al-Nūr (Qur'ān 24:11)

Betrayal hurts, but it teaches us not to be too trusting.

Breakups hurt, but they teach us that setting boundaries is important.

A lot of other things hurt, too, but the difficult situations we encounter in life teach us to be stronger.

All of the pain and suffering the believers are exposed to becomes an **expiation for their sins** as they draw closer to Allāh ﷻ, because these situations remind us that it is Allāh ﷻ alone upon Whom we rely and trust—**and all this is good nourishment for the believer's soul.**

فَوَيْلٌ لِّلْقَٰسِيَةِ قُلُوبُهُم مِّن ذِكْرِ ٱللَّهِ

Fa-waylun li-l-qāsiyati qulūbuhum min dhikri llāh

"Then woe to those whose hearts are hardened against the remembrance of Allāh."

— *Sūrat al-Zumar (Qur'ān 39:22)*

My friend,

Nothing is worth grieving over so long as the light of Allāh ﷻ glows in your heart, but if one chooses the path of darkness and rejects His guidance, that will be a path of sorrow, loss, and regret, putting one into a state of clear or "manifest" error, as Allāh ﷻ says in the same verse.

Deliberately rejecting goodness and choosing to go astray results in the destruction of the heart, mind, and soul, which were originally designed (by Allāh's mercy) to believe in Allah's words and be touched by them.

"Allāh has sent down the best statement: a consistent Book wherein is reiteration. The skins shiver therefrom of those who fear their Lord; then their skins and their hearts relax at the remembrance [i.e., mention] of Allāh. That is the guidance of Allāh by which He guides whom He wills. And one whom Allāh sends astray - for him there is no guide."[54]

Remember that Allāh ﷻ never sends someone astray unless

54. Qur'ān 39:23.

that person continuously rejects all forms of guidance, and this is the worst punishment one could ever have.

ٱلْمَالُ وَٱلْبَنُونَ زِينَةُ ٱلْحَيَوٰةِ ٱلدُّنْيَا

L-mālu wa-l-banūna zīnatu l-ḥayāti d-dunyā

"Wealth and children are [but] adornment of the worldly life."

— *Sūrat al-Kahf (Qur'ān 18:46)*

Don't let wealth and children be your only goals in life, as Allāh ﷻ tells us in the same verse that "the enduring good deeds are better to your Lord for reward and better for [one's] hope."[55]

Enduring good deeds are those that continue to benefit you even after you have departed from this world.

But is it possible to combine the temporary adornments of this life with enduring good deeds?

Yes, of course. When you raise your children to be good Muslims and use your wealth in a way that is pleasing to Allāh ﷻ, this will surely be of benefit to you in the Hereafter.

But one should realize that **these two things in particular (wealth and children) are a "fitnah (trial)"**[56] for humankind, because they can lead to pride, heedlessness, arrogance, and extravagance if we allow this worldly life to delude us with its temptations.

55. Qur'ān 18:46.

56. Qur'ān 8:28.

وَمَا ٱلْحَيَوٰةُ ٱلدُّنْيَآ إِلَّا مَتَـٰعُ ٱلْغُرُورِ

Wa-mā l-ḥayātu d-dunyā ʾillā matāʿu l-ghurūr

"And what is the worldly life except the enjoyment of delusion."

— Sūrat al-Ḥadīd (Qurʾān 57:20)

In the same verse quoted from above, Allāh ﷻ describes the worldly pleasures of this life as "the example of a rain whose [resulting] plant growth pleases the tillers,"[57] which soon "withers." After this, "you see it turned yellow; then it becomes [scattered] debris."

Do your best to invest your efforts into a harvest that **never goes to waste or withers away and dies.**

And remember...

"Whoever desires the harvest of the Hereafter - We [Allāh ﷻ] increase for him in his harvest [i.e., reward]. And whoever desires the harvest [i.e., benefits] of this world - We give him thereof, but there is not for him in the Hereafter any share."[58]

57. Those who cultivate the land.

58. Qurʾān 42:20.

قَالَ يَٰبُنَيَّ لَا تَقۡصُصۡ رُءۡيَاكَ عَلَىٰٓ إِخۡوَتِكَ فَيَكِيدُواْ لَكَ كَيۡدًا

Qāla yā-bunayya lā taqṣuṣ ru'yāka 'alā 'ikhwatika fa-yakīdū laka kaydā

"He said, 'O my son, do not relate your vision to your brothers or they will contrive against you a plan.'"

— *Sūrat Yūsuf (Qur'ān 12:5)*

How much do you tell others?

Whom do you trust with your innermost thoughts and feelings, your happy moments, your little successes, and your good news?

Some or all of these things should undoubtedly remain private (or confined to a few trusted people), yet it has become a habit in today's world to overshare.

Remember that some people will feel jealous, unappreciative, or envious, and some may even try to hurt you, even if only with their words.

Choose the people you trust carefully, as not everyone should be given access to the unique treasures of your heart—**but be respectful to everyone without exceptions.**

وَلَقَدْ نَعْلَمُ أَنَّكَ يَضِيقُ صَدْرُكَ بِمَا يَقُولُونَ

Wa-la-qad naʿlamu ʾannaka yaḍīqu ṣadruka bi-mā yaqūlūn

"And We already know that your breast is constrained by what they say."

— Sūrat al-Ḥijr (Qurʾān 15:97)

Regardless of whether it happens in person or online, **do not go down to the same level** if you are ever distressed by someone's speech.

Remember that Allāh ﷻ knows and hears all that takes place, so "exalt [Allāh] with praise of your Lord and be of those who prostrate [to Him]."[59]

This is the best cure from Allāh ﷻ for this type of annoyance.

59. Qurʾān 15:98.

بَلِ ٱلْإِنسَٰنُ عَلَىٰ نَفْسِهِۦ بَصِيرَةٌ

Bali l-ʾinsānu ʿalā nafsihī baṣīrah

"Rather, man, against himself, will be a witness."

— *Sūrat al-Qiyāmah (Qurʾān 75:14)*

Just as your body knows what is best for its physical health, it also knows what is best for it from a spiritual perspective.

Through *fiṭrah* (the innate disposition toward goodness and *tawḥīd*[60] we have all been created with):

- Your heart longs for the remembrance of Allāh ﷻ;
- Your eyes seek the pleasure that comes with contemplating the beauty of Allāh's creations;
- Your tongue dislikes idle talk;
- Your ears are content with Allāh's words;
- Your hands love to work for the benefit of others;
- Your feet dislike visiting places of corruption.

Do you recognize and nourish the above—or have you deprived yourself from the peace that comes from meeting your body's spiritual needs?

Allāh ﷻ informs us in the Qurʾān that our organs and other body parts **will speak to Him ﷻ on the Day of Judgement and testify about what we made them do in this life.**[61]

60. Belief in One God.

61. Qurʾān 36:65.

ٱلْمُؤْمِنُونَ وَٱلْمُؤْمِنَٰتُ بَعْضُهُمْ أَوْلِيَآءُ بَعْضٍ

Al-mu'minūna wa-l-mu'minātu ba'ḍuhum 'awliyā'u ba'ḍ

"The believing men and believing women are allies of one another."

— *Sūrat al-Tawbah (Qur'ān 9:71)*

To every woman who has a husband:

Be an ally to your husband through your patience and supportive words.

There were many times when Prophet Muḥammad ﷺ and his wife 'Ā'ishah (RA) had nothing more than dates and water at home, but 'Ā'ishah (RA) never complained or burdened the Prophet ﷺ and always patiently made the best out of what they had.

Whether you make your own money or depend on your husband's salary, don't go spending it on everything that your heart desires without any thought to financial planning.

It is true that your husband is the one responsible for supporting the family, but you will be rewarded by Allāh ﷻ when you show wisdom in spending and alleviate some of the stress he feels as a provider.

Just as you feel happy when your efforts are recognized and

appreciated by your husband, your husband feels the same way when his efforts are appreciated and recognized by you.

Remember that the two of you are a team with important goals in common!

Be a helping hand to one another as you strive for Jannah; this way, when one hand weakens, the other will strengthen it to bring it back on track. This is how the believers show allegiance to each other, whether they are colleagues, siblings, spouses, or friends.

وَٱللَّهُ أَحَقُّ أَن تَخۡشَىٰهُ

Wa-llāhu 'aḥaqqu 'an takhshāh

"While Allāh has more right that you fear Him."

— *Sūrat al-Aḥzāb (Qur'ān 33:37)*

Don't let social norms make you allow what has been prohibited by Allāh ﷻ or even prohibit what has been allowed.

We should also be cautious about what we do or don't do out of fear of people's judgment, as it is Allāh ﷻ alone to Whom we are accountable, and He is much more worthy of our fear, respect, and consideration in all areas of life.

This is also true when it comes to acts of worship and other praiseworthy deeds. We should do these purely for the sake of Allāh ﷻ, and not because we are afraid that others will criticize us if we don't do them.

But even if you sometimes worry that you are not fully sincere about your intentions, do not stop doing the good things that you are doing, as this is one of the deceptive tactics used by Satan to divert humankind away from the path of guidance.

Always maintain your prayers and continue to do good deeds, no matter what, but take your occasional doubts as a sign from Allāh ﷻ that you should work to improve your knowledge of Islām and further strengthen your relationship with Allāh ﷻ.

You can do this by always asking Allāh ﷻ to guide you and making the effort to learn His many names and what each of His descriptive traits means on a deeper level.

Read more about Islām from trustworthy sources so that you gain more understanding of His commands and prohibitions.

Most importantly, learn what the Most Merciful Creator actually says in His Holy Book, the Glorious Qur'ān, which He describes in the Qur'ān itself as "healing and mercy for the believers."[62]

62. Qur'ān 17:82.

وَتَوَاصَوْا۟ بِٱلْحَقِّ وَتَوَاصَوْا۟ بِٱلصَّبْرِ

Wa-tawāṣaw bi-l-ḥaqqi wa-tawāṣaw bi-ṣ-ṣabr

"...And advised each other to truth and advised each other to patience."

— *Sūrat al-ʿAṣr (Qurʾān 103:3)*

To be excluded from a state of loss, as Allāh ﷻ tells us in the same chapter of the Qurʾān, it is not enough to be a believer who does good deeds. **We should also care about one another and advise each other.**

Your advice can take many different forms.

It could be by sharing an enlightening short video, or by writing an article or post on social media.

And of course, never underestimate the impact of good words you utter right on spot to someone with a grieving heart.

وَهُدُوٓاْ إِلَى ٱلطَّيِّبِ مِنَ ٱلْقَوْلِ وَهُدُوٓاْ إِلَىٰ صِرَٰطِ ٱلْحَمِيدِ

Wa-hudū ʾilā ṭ-ṭayyibi mina l-qawli wa-hudū ʾilā ṣirāṭi l-ḥamīd

"And they had been guided [in worldly life] to good speech, and they were guided to the path of the Praiseworthy."

— *Sūrat al-Ḥajj (Qurʾān 22:24)*

Notice how Allāh ﷻ gives so much importance to the way we speak to others that He even made one's good speech in this worldly life **a means of attaining Paradise!**

The best place to learn this beautiful skill is contained within the stories of the prophets found in the Qurʾān.

Focus on the verses that show how they spoke with the disbelievers, and imagine yourself in the same situations.

They were relentlessly denied, mocked, ridiculed, and threatened.

Yet they always managed to maintain a tone of respect, patience, kindness, and wisdom in their speech.

What about you? How do you speak during your ordinary everyday conversations? And what tone do you use with others when conversing online?

Let this be your motto:

If it isn't appropriate during everyday face-to-face interactions, then it isn't appropriate on social media, either.

Remember that the people you are speaking to are often mothers, fathers, and grandparents. But even if they are not, people may be deeply affected by your words, and thus your words should always be chosen with care.

O Allāh, guide us to be among those who always weigh their words before speaking or writing...

فَتَبَيَّنُوٓاْ أَن تُصِيبُواْ قَوۡمَۢا بِجَهَٰلَةٖ

Fa-tabayyanū 'an tuṣībū qawman bi-jahālah

"Investigate, lest you harm a people out of ignorance."

— *Sūrat al-Ḥujurāt (Qur'ān 49:6)*

In other words, **don't believe everything you hear.** This was an important lesson for the early Muslims fourteen centuries ago, so how about now when almost everything we see on the Internet is fake news?

How many times did a video go viral before we realized it was fabricated?

How many times were someone's words taken out of context in order to create a huge scandal?

How many times were people bullied online for something they did not even say or do?

Is that not harming people?

Make it a habit not to comment on everything you see online, especially when the matter does not directly concern you.

More importantly, do not share news with others before you verify it is true from an authentic source.

Keep in mind that commenting on videos, articles, and social media posts helps them proliferate on a wider scale, and we don't want to be the reason for causing more harm.

يَٰٓأَيُّهَا ٱلَّذِينَ ءَامَنُوا۟ لَا يَسْخَرْ قَوْمٌ مِّن قَوْمٍ عَسَىٰٓ أَن يَكُونُوا۟ خَيْرًا مِّنْهُمْ

Yā-ʾayyuhā lladhīna ʾāmanū lā yaskhar qawmun min qawmin ʿasā ʾan yakūnū khayran minhum

"O you who have believed, let not a people ridicule [another] people; perhaps they may be better than them."

— *Sūrat al-Ḥujurāt (Qurʾān 49:11)*

Remember this whenever you feel the urge to insult, mock, or backbite someone.

Allāh ﷻ does not give importance to our skin color, race, social status, or physical appearance.

To the contrary, Allāh ﷻ tells us: **"The most noble of you in the sight of Allāh is the most righteous."**[63]

63. Qurʾān 49:13.

إِنَّ ٱللَّهَ لَا يُغَيِّرُ مَا بِقَوْمٍ حَتَّىٰ يُغَيِّرُوا۟ مَا بِأَنفُسِهِمْ

ʾInna llāha lā yughayyiru mā bi-qawmin ḥattā yughayyirū mā bi-ʾanfusihim

"Indeed, Allāh will not change the condition of a people until they change what is in themselves."

— Sūrat al-Raʿd (Qurʾān 13:11)

Have you ever wondered how a certain person changed so drastically?

Whether the change was positive or negative, the secret lies in the little steps we talked about earlier.

If you wish for your situation to change for the better, stop waiting for a miracle to happen, and start working hard to create the conditions that will lead to this change—but don't forget to **rely on Allāh ﷻ first!**

سَلَٰمٌ عَلَيۡكُم بِمَا صَبَرۡتُمۡ فَنِعۡمَ عُقۡبَى ٱلدَّارِ

Salāmun ʿalaykum bi-mā ṣabartum
fa-niʿma ʿuqbā d-dār

"'Peace [i.e., security] be upon you for what you patiently endured.' And excellent is the final abode."

— *Sūrat al-Raʿd (Qurʾān 13:24)*

This will, *in shāʾ Allāh*, be how the believers are welcomed at the gates of Paradise...

Because creating positive change within ourselves wasn't easy, but we did it for the sake of Allāh ﷻ...

Because not responding to bad speech in the same manner we were addressed was frustrating, but we held back for the sake of Allāh ﷻ...

Because displeasing others for the sake of pleasing Allāh ﷻ was a hard choice, but we still did it...

And because worldly desires were extremely tempting, yet we left them aside for the sake of Allāh ﷻ.

Stay firm, and don't lose your determination.

كَفَىٰ بِٱللَّهِ شَهِيدًا بَيْنِي وَبَيْنَكُمْ وَمَنْ عِندَهُۥ عِلْمُ ٱلْكِتَٰبِ

Kafā bi-llāhi shahīdan baynī wa-baynakum
wa-man ʿindahū ʿilmu l-kitāb

"Sufficient is Allāh as Witness between me and you, and [the witness of] whoever has knowledge of the Scripture."

— *Sūrat al-Raʿd (Qurʾān 13:43)*

This is an answer to the followers of other heavenly revealed religions who deny the prophethood of Prophet Muḥammad ﷺ.

The true knowers of their scriptures who take it upon themselves to study Islām in a sincere and dedicated manner can't but recognize that the Qurʾān is indeed **the final comprehensive truth revealed by their Lord to humankind.** This is actually a common experience among converts to Islām, who often embrace the religion after evaluating the details of other scriptures as compared to the Qurʾān.

Knowledge rather than emotion is the key to true faith.

To anyone who did not yet discover Islām:

Let this be your motivation to gain more insight into the faith followed by nearly two billion people (about a fourth of the world's population). Your life is more worthy than following a wrong religion, or no religion at all, while the truth was so close to you the whole time...

وَٱصۡبِرۡ لِحُكۡمِ رَبِّكَ فَإِنَّكَ بِأَعۡيُنِنَا

Wa-ṣbir li-ḥukmi rabbika fa-ʾinnaka bi-ʾaʿyuninā

"And be patient for the decision of your Lord, for indeed, you are in Our eyes [i.e., sight]."

— Sūrat al-Ṭūr (Qurʾān 52:48)

A heartfelt story that comes to mind when reading this verse is the story of Yūsuf (PBUH).

When Yūsuf (PBUH) told his father Yaʿqūb (PBUH) about a strange dream he had,[64] his father was keen on protecting his son from his envious siblings.

But Allāh ﷻ willed for Yūsuf (PBUH) to go through the experience of being thrown into a well by his brothers and then picked up by some travelers and sold to al-ʿAzīz (the minister in charge of supplies in Egypt), eventually ending up in prison on false charges, and remaining there for several years before the truth was finally revealed and Yūsuf (PBUH) was acquitted and appointed by the king to a respectable position in recognition of his knowledge and trustworthiness. Just after that, Yūsuf (PBUH) was finally reunited with Yaʿqūb (PBUH) after confronting his brothers.

When Yūsuf (PBUH) finally met with his elderly father, Yūsuf (PBUH) told him:

64. Qurʾān 12:4–6.

"O my father, this is the explanation of my vision of before. My Lord has made it reality. And He was certainly good to me when He took me out of prison and brought you [here] out of the desert after Satan had induced [estrangement] between me and my brothers. Indeed, my Lord is Subtle in what He wills. Indeed, it is He who is the Knowing, the Wise."[65]

"Subtle in what He wills" means that it may be Allāh's will for unexpected good things to come out of situations that are initially very difficult, painful, or distressing.

So, in the midst of all the chaos and undesired mess we sometimes find ourselves in, never forget that you are indeed **in His sight.**

65. Qur'ān 12:100.

إِنَّمَآ أَشۡكُواْ بَثِّي وَحُزۡنِيٓ إِلَى ٱللَّهِ

ʾInnamā ʾashkū baththī wa-ḥuznī ʾilā llāh

"I only complain of my suffering and my grief to Allāh."

— *Sūrat Yūsuf (Qurʾān 12:86)*

Although it was very distressing for Yaʿqūb (PBUH) to be separated from Yūsuf (PBUH), not even knowing where he was for many years, he never questioned the wisdom of Allāh ﷻ, nor did he ever doubt His existence or mercy.

He did not even ask anyone for help.

He instead went to Allāh ﷻ with all of his sadness.

We can say that a person with the patience of Yaʿqūb (PBUH) truly knows Allāh ﷻ, truly loves Allāh ﷻ, and truly trusts in Allāh ﷻ.

When devastating situations burden your soul, speak to Him, cry to Him, and **trust in Him ﷻ.**

No one will truly understand what you are going through but Him ﷻ, and **in His hands alone is your relief.**

فَلَا يَحْزُنكَ قَوْلُهُمْ

Fa-lā yaḥzunka qawluhum

"So let not their speech grieve you."

— *Sūrat Yā-Sīn (Qur'ān 36:76)*

Recite this verse whenever you feel saddened by someone's words.

Allāh ﷻ does not like for you to be sad.

The Great and Merciful Creator Himself is spoken about in negative terms by ignorant and ungrateful people who even deny His existence, but does that take away from Allāh's greatness or power even a tiny bit?

Did the prophets (peace be upon them all) start doubting themselves when others mocked them?

Keep your head high.

وَتِلْكَ ٱلْأَيَّامُ نُدَاوِلُهَا بَيْنَ ٱلنَّاسِ

Wa-tilka l-ʾayyāmu nudāwiluhā bayna n-nās

"And these days [of varying conditions] We alternate among the people."

— *Sūrat Āli ʿImrān (Qurʾān 3:140)*

Life is full of trials, with ups and downs in all spheres of our existence that may affect one mentally or physically as we experience changes to our health, living conditions, financial status, interpersonal relationships, and more.

Even the quality of one's faith may increase and decrease at different points in our lives.

So, don't be too sad or too happy—and never think you are immune from experiencing a certain situation.

To protect your heart during times of fluctuation, recite this supplication:

"Our Lord, let not our hearts deviate after You have guided us, and grant us from Yourself mercy."[66]

These varying conditions are actually tests "so that Allāh may make evident those who believe."[67]

66. Qurʾān 3:8.

67. Qurʾān 3:140.

"Or do you think that you will enter Paradise while Allāh has not yet made evident those of you who fight in His cause and made evident those who are steadfast?"[68]

68. Qur'ān 3:142.

وَمَنْ أَعْرَضَ عَن ذِكْرِي فَإِنَّ لَهُۥ مَعِيشَةً ضَنكًا

Wa-man ʾaʿraḍa ʿan dhikrī fa-ʾinna lahū maʿīshatan ḍankā

"And whoever turns away from My remembrance - indeed, he will have a depressed [i.e., difficult] life."

— Sūrat Ṭā-Hā (Qur'ān 20:124)

In addition to a number of other reasons, **Allāh ﷻ revealed the Qur'ān to make this life bearable for humankind.**

His words in the Qur'ān confirm His existence and remind us that He is there for us—to answer our supplications, to comfort us, and to accept our repentance. His words give us hope and assure us that we were indeed created for a noble reason.

This verse tells us that those who arrogantly turn away from remembrance of the Creator and seek other sources of relief for what ails the soul instead finding comfort with the remembrance of Allāh ﷻ will never find contentment or meaning in life no matter how hard they try, and this will ultimately lead to misery in the Hereafter as well.

After this, Allāh ﷻ tells us:

"We will gather [i.e., raise] him on the Day of Resurrection blind."[69]

69. Qur'ān 20:124.

"He will say, 'My Lord, why have you raised me blind while I was [once] seeing?'"[70]

"[Allāh] will say, 'Thus did Our signs come to you, and you forgot [i.e., disregarded] them; and thus will you this Day be forgotten.'"[71]

O Allāh, let us be among those who recognize Your signs and turn to You.

70. Qur'ān 20:125.

71. Qur'ān 20:126.

لَقَدۡ خَلَقۡنَا ٱلۡإِنسَٰنَ فِيٓ أَحۡسَنِ تَقۡوِيمٍ

La-qad khalaqnā l-ʾinsāna fī ʾaḥsani taqwīm

"We have certainly created man in the best of stature."

— *Sūrat al-Tīn (Qur'ān 95:4)*

Humankind is different from other His other creations.

Allāh ﷻ created us to walk upright, with symmetrical features that are balanced in form and nature. Our brains allow us to think, reason, comprehend our surroundings, and exchange thoughts with others.

He further provided us with the ability to choose and judge.

And He gave us emotions.

He granted us all of the tools one could ever need to make this world a better place, to be of help to others, and to represent the religion He entrusted us with as Muslims.

وَأَمَّا مَا يَنفَعُ ٱلنَّاسَ فَيَمۡكُثُ فِي ٱلۡأَرۡضِ

Wa-ʾammā mā yanfaʿu n-nāsa fa-yamkuthu fī l-ʾarḍ

"But as for that which benefits the people, it remains on the earth."

— *Sūrat al-Raʿd (Qurʾān 13:17)*

Beneficial knowledge, good deeds, and acts of perpetual charity are the things that remain, while anything non-beneficial that encourages corruption eventually fades away, even if it outshines goodness for a brief period.

Allāh ﷻ describes falsehood in the same verse as foam or "froth" that eventually vanishes, "cast off" from the clear water it has temporarily clouded.

We see this clearly in today's popular trends, which will undoubtedly be gone just as quickly as they started, with no benefit gained at all—yet there is always a certain number of people who ride on the waves of such trends regardless of how vulgar or ridiculous they actually are.

Don't let your valuable time be occupied with these distractions; instead aim to have **a record rich with everlasting good deeds.**

وَكُنَّا نَخُوضُ مَعَ ٱلْخَآئِضِينَ

Wa-kunnā nakhūḍu ma'a l-khā'iḍīn

"And we used to enter into vain discourse with those who engaged [in it]."

— *Sūrat al-Muddaththir (Qur'ān 74:45)*

In a state of regret, this will be among the confessions of those who did not work for their Hereafter as they acknowledge their wrongdoings, saying: "We were not of those who prayed, nor did we used to feed the poor, **and we used to enter into vain discourse with those who engaged [in it].**"[72]

Not every discussion is worth having, not every piece of news is worth following, and not every spectacle is worth watching.

Fill your time with the remembrance of Allāh ﷻ **in order to attain success in the Hereafter.**

Even when you are having fun with friends and family, strive to make your time together beneficial and pleasing to Allāh ﷻ.

72. Qur'ān 74:43-45.

مِنۡهَا خَلَقۡنَٰكُمۡ وَفِيهَا نُعِيدُكُمۡ

Minhā khalaqnākum wa-fīhā nuʿīdukum

"From it [i.e., the earth] We created you, and into it We will return you."

— Sūrat Ṭā-Hā (Qur'ān 20:55)

Don't allow the dazzling lights of this worldly life to blind your eyes from the inevitable reality described in this verse.

Make it a habit every once in a while to visit the graves of the Muslims and recite this supplication taught to us by Prophet Muḥammad ﷺ: "Peace be upon you, O inmates of the graves. May Allāh ﷻ forgive us and you. **You have preceded us, and we are to follow.**"[73]

73. *Riyāḍ al-Ṣāliḥīn, No. 583.*

رَبَّنَا ٱغْفِرْ لَنَا وَلِإِخْوَٰنِنَا ٱلَّذِينَ سَبَقُونَا بِٱلْإِيمَٰنِ

Rabbanā ghfir lanā wa-li-ʾikhwāninā lladhīna sabaqūnā bi-l-ʾīmān

"Our Lord, forgive us and our brothers who preceded us in faith."

— Sūrat Al-Ḥashr (Qurʾān 59:10)

Supplicate for yourself...

And for your parents and your grandparents...

And for your teachers and your uncles and aunts...

And for the people whom you know or deal with in your everyday life...

And for those in the public eye who've inspired you to become a better person, such as television hosts, authors, and others...

And for strangers...

And for the oppressed...

And for scholars...

And for those who have already left this world...

And for the prophets (peace be upon them) and the noble Companions of Prophet Muḥammad ﷺ (may Allāh be pleased with them all).

Sincere love and appreciation for the people whom you claim to like or care about is revealed when you supplicate for them to Allāh ﷻ without their knowledge.

But the purest form of love is the love that makes you wish goodness for all of humanity, including all of your Muslim brothers and sisters as well as the non-Muslims of this world (by praying for their guidance).

And this is all an expression of faith.

وَلَا تَجْعَلْ فِي قُلُوبِنَا غِلًّا لِّلَّذِينَ ءَامَنُوا

Wa-lā taj'al fī qulūbinā ghillan li-lladhīna 'āmanū

"And put not in our hearts [any] resentment toward those who have believed."

— *Sūrat Al-Ḥashr (Qur'ān 59:10)*

"No one of you becomes a true believer until he likes for his brother what he likes for himself."[74]

Never forget that there is a special bond between you and your Muslim brothers and sisters in faith.

Always aim to purify your heart from any malicious feelings, such as envy, hatred, or jealousy toward anyone. Even if someone hurts you with their harsh words, be better than that person. Don't hold grudges—and simply leave the matter to Allāh ﷻ.

Be like a sweet breeze that only spreads good feelings among people, and focus on their positive qualities when dealing with them, wishing them every goodness from Allāh ﷻ, including the blessings of His guidance.

74. A saying of Prophet Muḥammad ﷺ (*Riyāḍ al-Ṣāliḥīn*, No. 183).

وَمَا مِن دَآبَّةٍ فِي ٱلۡأَرۡضِ إِلَّا عَلَى ٱللَّهِ رِزۡقُهَا وَيَعۡلَمُ مُسۡتَقَرَّهَا
وَمُسۡتَوۡدَعَهَاۚ كُلّٞ فِي كِتَٰبٖ مُّبِينٖ

Wa-mā min dābbatin fī l-ʾarḍi ʾillā ʿalā llāhi
rizquhā wa-yaʿlamu mustaqarrahā
wa-mustawdaʿahā kullun fī kitābin mubīn

"And there is no creature on earth but that upon Allāh is its provision, and He knows its place of dwelling and place of storage.[75] All is in a clear register."

— Sūrat Hūd (Qurʾān 11:6)

All of His creations are provided for, whether they are wild animals or birds, domesticated flocks, ants, bees, and other tiny insects and creatures that we are not even aware of.

Glory be to Allāh! Do you then think that the Most Merciful Creator would ever abandon humankind, leaving us lost with no guidance or provision?

Let this be your motivation to **work with faith, contentment, and belief.**

75. Before birth and after death.

لَا يُكَلِّفُ ٱللَّهُ نَفْسًا إِلَّا وُسْعَهَا

Lā yukallifu llāhu nafsan ʾillā wusʿahā

"Allāh does not charge a soul except [with that within] its capacity."

— *Sūrat al-Baqarah (Qurʾān 2:286)*

Allāh ﷻ will never put you in a situation that you can't handle.

Even when it comes to acts of worship that may seem difficult at first, Allāh ﷻ knows that we are capable of doing them and has prescribed them for our own benefit.

Fasting, for example, requires a great deal of patience and self-discipline, but it teaches us that we actually possess many hidden abilities that we have not discovered or tapped into yet. We also learn that it is not impossible to build healthy habits.

Prayer requires strict adherence to a particular schedule, but it also shows us that we can organize our affairs and achieve balance between the different facets of our lives.

Compare these examples to other matters in your life that seem difficult, including any hardships or tests you may be facing. Aim to handle such challenges with a positive attitude of strength and patience as you **extract the lessons from each situation in order to enhance the quality of your life.**

And remember...

You've got this!

أَلَمْ يَعْلَم بِأَنَّ ٱللَّهَ يَرَىٰ

ʾA-lam yaʿlam bi-ʾanna llāha yarā

"Does he not know that Allāh sees?"

— *Sūrat al-ʿAlaq (Qurʾān 96:14)*

Does "he" not know that Allāh sees?

That person who cheats others...

Who neglects his responsibilities...

Who won't say a word of truth...

Who lives in hypocrisy according to what best serves his interests...

Who goes with the flow even when the flow is corruption...

Who hurts others with his actions and words...

Who calls for immorality and lies...

Is "he" not afraid of The Most Just?

In *Sūrat al-Muʾminūn* (Chapter 23 of the Qurʾān), Allāh ﷻ tells us about the moment when all of humanity will come back to life after everyone on Earth has died. At that time, Allāh ﷻ will say:

"Then did you think that We created you uselessly and that to Us you would not be returned? So exalted is Allāh, the Sovereign, the Truth; there is no deity except Him, **Lord of the Noble Throne.**"[76]

76. Qurʾān 23:115–116.

فَمَن يَعۡمَلۡ مِثۡقَالَ ذَرَّةٍ خَيۡرٗا يَرَهُۥ

Fa-man yaʿmal mithqāla dharratin khayran yarah

"So whoever does an atom's weight[77] of good will see it."

— Sūrat al-Zalzalah (Qur'ān 99:7)

Let this verse serve as both a reminder and your best motivation for doing good deeds.

It is reassurance from Allāh ﷻ that **anything done for purely for His sake will never go to waste.**

Imagine your feeling when you see the rewards you have attained for everything good you have done in this life on The Day on Judgment, when even the tiniest act of goodness toward another creation of Allāh ﷻ will weigh heavily on your scale of good deeds.

So, strive for increased goodness, and don't let laziness defeat you.

77. Or "the weight of a small ant."

Author's Note and Conclusion

Dear reader,

Now that we have gone through this marvelous journey together of delving into some verses from Allāh's Holy Book, let us reflect on what we have learned so that we may create positive changes in our lives in order to become better Muslims, *in shā' Allāh*.

Below is a practical exercise that we can all participate in—including me, you, the members of your household, your friends, and anyone else you may know. It is also a fun and motivational activity that you may wish to organize for the Muslim children and teens in your community.

STEP ONE: Each participant should create two separate lists with the following headings:

- Things I would like to improve in my private relationship with Allāh ﷻ;
- Things I would like to improve in my relationships with people.

STEP TWO: After this, brainstorm as many ideas as possible, placing each one under the appropriate heading from STEP ONE above. Some examples may include goals such as the following:

- Praying the five obligatory prayers on time;
- Praying the *sunnah* prayers;
- Waking up for Fajr every day;
- Voluntarily fasting throughout the year;

- Reciting morning and night *dhikr*;
- Dressing more modestly;
- Giving more charity;
- Making the effort to study the meanings of Allāh's verses;
- Memorizing more Qur'ān;
- Making it a habit to smile;
- Listening attentively when someone else is speaking;
- Focusing on people's good qualities rather than backbiting them;
- Spending more time with parents and family;
- Checking on people more frequently, including aunts, uncles, and others;
- Your own creative ideas.

STEP THREE: Now that you have created two robust and meaningful lists, choose **just one item** from each category that you wish to focus on and remain committed to.

For example, perhaps your goal with Allāh ﷻ is to maintain the five obligatory prayers, while your goal with people is to refrain from backbiting.

The reason we are only choosing one item from each category is so that we successfully cultivate habitual changes that we permanently maintain, *in shā' Allāh*, without overwhelming ourselves in the process. Keep in mind the words of Prophet Muḥammad ﷺ, who said:

"The acts most pleasing to Allāh are those which are done continuously, even if they are small."[78]

78. *Ṣaḥīḥ Muslim*, No. 258.

STEP FOUR: Write the above *ḥadīth* at the start of a calendar that you dedicate for this purpose. If you are able to do so, you may wish to include the original Arabic wording as well:

«أَحَبُّ الْأَعْمَالِ إِلَى اللهِ أدومها وَإِن قل.»

STEP FIVE: Starting from today, mark each day that you commit to the two new habitual changes with a small sticker or check-mark, and challenge yourself to continue doing these two things for a whole year.

STEP SIX: In addition to the above, commit to doing one random good deed on a daily basis, and make note of it on your calendar each day. This can be something good that you do for others, or even for yourself. Examples of simple good deeds may include the following:

- Visiting an elderly neighbor or relative;
- Helping someone with a task;
- Teaching a child;
- Bringing someone a gift;
- Watering plants;
- Feeding an animal;
- Writing something inspirational online;
- Taking care of your mental health;
- Your own creative ideas (you're going to need a lot of them for this activity).

STEP SEVEN: After a year passes, choose two new goals from the first two lists, and continue with your daily good deeds as well.

Aim to continue with this strategy for as long as you are alive.

Before you know it, you will have become a new person who loves Allāh ﷻ even more than you already did. By His will, you will also feel the glow of Allāh's light in your life as you continue to strive for His sake.

May Allāh ﷻ bless you, whoever and wherever you are.

Printed in Great Britain
by Amazon

51098384R00091